GH00976283

First published in Ireland by Greatfood.ie 2010.
Greatfood.ie, 17 Rathfarnham Road, Terenure, Dublin 6, Ireland.
www.greatfood.ie

Editor: Anne Kennedy
Photography: Harry Weir
Art Direction and Design: Anne Kennedy and Liezel Schultz
Recipe Testing: Marco Roccasalvo

ISBN 978-0956652102

Printer: Digiprint.ie, Dublin, Ireland. www.digiprint.ie

Richard,
Thanks for your kindness and
coffee + sustenance when
I edited the book "Spoon".

Anne

GRADASSI
CAMPELLO SUL CLITUNNO
TRADIZIONE FAMILIARE
DAL *1639*

MOAK®

digiprint·ie
print & design

DUBLINO Istituto Italiano di Cultura   DUBLINO Istituto Italiano di Cultura

With the patronage of the Italian Institute of Culture, Dublin.

Inside The Italian Kitchen

Marco Roccasalvo and Anne Kennedy

PHOTOGRAPHS *by* Harry Weir

greatfood.ie

INTRODUCTION

When Marco Roccasalvo arrived in Ireland almost ten years ago, he was a relative latecomer to the Italian food scene. In some ways he reaped the benefits of that belated arrival. When he opened his restaurant *Campo de' Fiori* in the seaside town of Bray outside Dublin and politely but firmly refused to add cream to sauces or to make *Spaghetti alla Carbonara* with white wine, people were surprised but they did not reject him out of hand. Over time, they returned to experiment and slowly but surely he nurtured a growing and loyal band of customers who came to appreciate that authentic Italian food, the food that Italians actually eat in their own country, is simply much better than its confused Irish cousin.

At *Campo de' Fiori* Marco and his team have created a destination restaurant where you can find a real taste of Italy. People come from all over the city and its environs to eat hand-cut cured meats, to see what Marco can do with a fresh lobster and a handful of pasta, to enjoy a restrained *Fiorentina* adorned with just olive oil and salt and to explore regional dishes that he has researched first-hand. Marco's quiet strength of purpose and the genial way he sells what may at first appear to be a lack of compromise works to his advantage. In the early days, had he wavered when he was asked to cook a quick dish of *penne* with chicken and mushroom 'just to please the wife' he would have lost the high moral ground not just as a chef but for the Italian cuisine. Instead, he took the time to explain what real Italian food should be. By the time he finished, his guests were truly charmed and ready to try his suggestions. This approach takes time and effort and when you are both chef and owner it can be a risky endeavour. (Many people would, with justification, ask who is this *eejit* who is turning away good money?) But Marco held firm and by doing so he has shown that there is space for a restaurant where you can weave delicious ingredients into joy on the plate.

The idea of this book emerged as a result of many conversations between Marco and I as to why Italian food, one of the oldest cuisines in the world, was not true to itself in Ireland. The most difficult thing has been to draw out the essence of Italian cuisine and to present it as simple tenets so that you can make authentic Italian food at home. In Italy people rarely agree on the subject of food and no doubt, given that this book reflects the vision of just one Italian chef and the ingredients that inform his cooking, we will contribute to that robust discussion.

We hope that we can share some of the seminal moments that make Italian cooking what it should be, those small details that make the difference between an average dish and an excellent one. The recipes are genuine: Marco cooks them in his restaurant and he has tested them at home. If you think some of the recipes are too simple to be excellent, then his work is done. Throughout the book I have done my best not to lose Marco's voice and where it is essential to the story, I have not tidied up his English.

Inside the Italian Kitchen also sums up what we are about at Greatfood.ie: a belief that good food doesn't have to cost the earth and should be available to everyone. That when you have good ingredients and cook them with intelligence and affection you can make an exceptional plate of food that is greater than the sum of its parts. Most of all, we want to share not just good food, but great food.

We are delighted that the *Italian Institute of Culture* has endorsed the book. It is a formidable compliment and we thank them for their kindness and confidence in us.

We hope you enjoy reading and cooking from *Inside the Italian Kitchen*.

Anne Kennedy

greatfood.ie

CONTENTS

COOKING WAS SOMETHING THAT I STARTED *to feel*
when I was about seven or eight. I began making *gnocchi* or homemade
pasta, just mixing the ingredients as I saw my mother do it. I was very
happy. My mother cooked for the priests in the seminary so she was at
work all day. She was this big *mamma* looking after the trainee priests.
She is a very good cook. Thirty five years ago in Italy things were very
different. When we finished school we were just running in the street on
our own without a problem until my mother came home. I knew when
she did that there would be trouble because the kitchen was messy because
I was there, making pasta or cooking. She just couldn't understand it.

I was born in Rome and I lived in the city for 23 years until I moved
30 miles south of Rome. Every Sunday my mother made homemade
pasta and I would wake up to find her making *fettuccine* or *ravioli*. It was my
job to unravel the *fettuccine* after she cut it with a knife or to help sprinkle
the flour. It was the best moment for me. It was *bello* to be alive. The food
she was making was just for the family. My mother is Sicilian so that had
a huge influence on her cooking. And of course she moved to Rome when
she was 25 so then she cooked Roman food too. Lots of dishes in Rome
are cooked with artichokes when they are in season. We ate *Coda alla
Vaccinara* (beef tail, a classic Roman dish) and *Coratella con Carciofi*
(intestines cooked with onions and artichokes) which she would make for
a special occasion.

Our typical lunch or dinner was *Spaghetti al Pomodoro* or often she served white fish like *merluzzo* (cod). We had roast chicken and *insalata*, lots of salad. My mother (pictured to the right with my brother and I on her birthday) still lives in Rome and in her garden she grows salad, beans, *radicchio* and *pomodori*.

When I was a child, from April to September it was my duty after we finished playing football at the Oratory to come back and water the garden. Because I was little I wasn't allowed to pick the tomatoes or the vegetables because you had to choose the ripest ones. That was the best bit but my parents didn't think I would be able to judge: 'Is this ready. Is this not?'. My parents understood that the ripeness of fruit and vegetables is so important in Italian cooking. From April to September on the table in the Roccasalvo's house there were always home-grown vegetables. My father has green fingers. He still grows *peperoncini* and in every little corner of his garden he has planted herbs. Everywhere there is something growing that you can eat.

THE ITALIAN STORECUPBOARD

There are some fundamental but very simple ingredients that you need to cook authentic Italian food. With these you can make most things once you add the main ingredients.

You'll need extra virgin olive oil, salt, freshly ground black pepper, a few fresh herbs like rosemary, basil, sage and parsley, dried rosemary and dried oregano (I never use fresh oregano), dried and fresh chilli (fresh chilli is better), garlic, onions and vinegar. You need only a few pieces of kitchen equipment and a cooker with an oven to make everything in this book.

CHOOSE YOUR MAIN INGREDIENT

If I'm by the sea I look for fresh fish, if I'm in the city centre I will look for nice vegetables and meat. If I decide to have pasta with fresh tomatoes, I try to find the best tomatoes. If I can't find ripe tomatoes, I use tinned (see page 48 for advice on choosing a good tinned tomato). I always try to choose food that is in season.

As you go through the book I'll explain the qualities of each ingredient and how to choose it. Of course, you'll need a good recipe too and in this book you'll find some of my favourites that I have created along with classic dishes like *Spaghetti alla Carbonara* (recipe on page 114) that I will show you how to make properly. You will add to your storecupboard, layer on layer. If a recipe needs saffron, once you buy it, it is something that will stay in your kitchen and you can use it for other dishes. It's the same with anchovies and capers or nutmeg but the fundamental ingredients that you start with to make any Italian recipe will not change. They are all you need to make genuine Italian food.

YOUR EQUIPMENT

You'll need a large high saucepan to boil the water for the pasta that fits both short and long pasta (we call it a *pentola*) and a few smaller saucepans; a colander to drain the pasta; one or two stainless steel frying pans (I use a non-stick pan for fish and scrambled eggs) and a lid.

Of course, you'll need a knife and a wooden spoon and a chopping board and a pepper mill and a few other utensils that you have in your kitchen anyway. A few bowls to mix things and a scales to weigh ingredients for desserts and something to serve the food in. That's it.

THE IMPORTANCE OF INGREDIENTS

In my restaurant and at home I always begin my cooking with good ingredients. Why are ingredients so important in Italian cooking? Because it is impossible to create a miracle from bad ingredients. I'm not saying that having the best quality is important. That the ingredients have character is more important to me. If you start with bad ingredients you have no opportunity to make something impressive.

I'm Italian so I start cooking in my brain! If I make a pasta dish with a particular cheese, say one from Sicily, I think about the flavour of the pasta, the olive oil, the cheese. To research recipes and ingredients, I go to Italy and talk to the producers.

Because it's impossible for everyone to do this, in the next pages I'll tell you how to buy ingredients that will make a real difference to your Italian cooking. Because Italian dishes depend on so few ingredients, you need to choose them carefully. As long as you pay attention to the detail, that you buy the freshest cherry tomatoes or the finest tinned ones, an olive oil with character, a jar of capers in salt rather than those in vinegar for example, you can find what you need in the supermarket, in a convenience store and at the delicatessen.

EXTRA VIRGIN OLIVE OIL

The olive tree is my favourite tree. The shape of the trunk is like a sculpture. If you go to Puglia and pass by the village of Alberobello (*albero* means tree and *bello* means beautiful) and you go down to Lecce in the heel of Italy, you come into Salento which is the most important area for olive oil. (Puglia produces the most olive oil in Europe.) When you drive on the left or right side, you will find only olive trees. Every tree is completely different. Sometimes the shape is made by the wind, sometimes by the rock, it is like something that is suffering, like a tree that is crying. It's not like an ordinary tree. There is a connection between how much the olive tree has to struggle and the olive oil it creates. If you have a field of beautiful land with water and where the sun is right, the wind is not too strong, that makes the life too easy for the olive trees so what you get at the end is nothing special. When the tree suffers, if the olive tree needs to find its way through rock or to cling on to the side of a slope, it produces better olives and you get a special olive oil.

Extra virgin olive oil is, in my opinion, the bedrock of the Italian diet. There is nothing that you can replace it with. People outside of Italy think that Italian people buy only the most expensive olive oil but in the supermarket, you will find that extra virgin olive oil at a few euro a litre is the bestseller. For this price you will find an honest olive oil which is good for cooking or for dressing a salad. In Italian supermarkets and

shops, you can find a large section of *olio extra vergine* and a much smaller section of *olio di oliva* (this is olive oil that is not extra virgin. It is often called 'virgin olive oil' for marketing purposes outside of Italy but it is not really used by Italians). Extra virgin olive oil is the only oil that is extracted without chemicals so it is pure, that's why it is called 'virgin'.

At my restaurant I use only extra virgin olive oil to cook with, to dress salads and *bruschetta*, for fish, for meat and to make soups and to dress the soup before serving to give the last kick to the plate. I use *Gradassi Extra Virgin Olive Oil* because for my opinion, the quality is exactly what I need for my cooking.

What makes the difference in the olive oil is the variety of olives used and the process that is used to extract the oil from the olive. Extra virgin olive oil comes from the first pressing of the olive. To make the extra virgin olive oil, the olives can be handpicked or dropped into a net but they can't touch the ground. The olives have to be brought to the press within 24 hours and pressed within that time. Sometimes the producer adds a few leaves to the pressing to give a very green oil with a strong flavour. It is something that you see when you go to the *frantoio* (the olive press) when the oil comes out from the press: if the leaves have been added, you get a stronger colour green and the flavour is more robust. I like it because it tastes like tannin. It's bitter.

The acidity in the olives increases when the olives hit the ground or they are left in the basket for a few days and the only oil you can get from these olives is called *olio lampante* (lamp oil) because that was the oil that was used for lamps. Why should you not use it? Because the acidity is too high and it's not good for your health.

If I go into a supermarket how can I know if the oil is good or not? Well, there is no way to see it from the label. Here you can only see the origin and the variety of olives used. From the colour you can say nothing. The only thing to do is buy the bottle, take a spoon or a piece of bread to dip in the olive oil and taste it to see if you like it or not. You don't need to be a *connoisseur*. The difference in terms of price of *olio di oliva* and *olio extra vergine* is *niente*. It's not huge so use extra virgin olive oil for cooking.

Pomace oil or *olio di sansa* is the lowest grade of oil and it is chemically extracted from the pulp of the olives. It's the last product that you get from the olive and it is extracted with a chemical called *esano*. You find it being used in many restaurant kitchens but never in my kitchen. Every time you use pomace oil you need to use a lot of oil because you burn everything whereas if you use extra virgin olive oil, you use less oil. If you cook something in the oven like fish in pomace oil, after 15 minutes cooking the oil is completely dissolved, and what you find is a very bad

smell and the fish is dry. But if you cook it with extra virgin olive oil it is completely different, you find olive oil in the tray with a very good flavour. The meat of the fish is still moist. For my preference, I prefer olive oil from Puglia, Sicily, Tuscany, Liguria, Lazio and Umbria, of course, which is where the extra virgin olive oil from *Gradassi* that I use comes from.

COLOUR: If the olive oil is very green the olives used are young and not ripe enough. That doesn't mean that it is not good, it just means that the characteristics of the oil are different. It will have a long finish, it's something that stays on your tongue. When the olives are ripe enough the colour is more yellow than green and the flavour is smooth. In my restaurant I use the *Gradassi Primi Frutti* for cooking because it is very mild. In November for dressing salads we use the *Gradassi Novello* when it is in season. I use the *DOP Umbria* for meat and fish. I prefer olive oil that is made with young olives for dressing as it has a stronger character and is more pronounced. I use the olive oil made with ripe olives for cooking because it's smoother. And of course you can find young green olive oil and yellow olive oil from all over Italy. When you buy an olive oil, the bottle shouldn't be clear glass, it should be dark to protect the oil from light which oxidizes it and affects the flavour. When you see an olive oil bottle wrapped in silver foil, that usually means that the oil is of a good quality because the producer has invested money to protect it.

HERBS AND HOW TO USE THEM

To understand the story of how herbs are so magical in Italian cooking, we should look at just one recipe in this book, *Spaghetti al Fuoco* (see page 130) that a lady in the Eolie Islands in Sicily taught me to make. *Fuoco* means 'at the fire' so the dish has to be spicy. You don't cook the tomatoes: you just find the best ripe tomatoes, cut them in a bowl, mix them with dried oregano, fresh basil, fresh parsley, garlic, fresh chilli, extra virgin olive oil and *ricotta infornata* or baked ricotta. When you drain the pasta, you toss it in the bowl and the pasta is ready. You get all the flavours of the herbs in the tomatoes.

I use fresh herbs at the beginning of cooking, sometimes frying them with the *soffritto* (the base made with olive oil, garlic, onion, carrot and celery), then add more fresh herbs to add vitality at the end of cooking. When I use dried herbs I also add them at the beginning of cooking and I add fresh parsley or basil at the end of cooking to give a last kick to the dish.

Sometimes I mix herbs: when I make *bruschetta*, I use fresh parsley and basil and add dried oregano. If you add dried oregano to tomatoes, then add fresh basil to another plate of tomatoes, the taste is completely different. That's the power of just a few grams of herbs.

OREGANO: I use only dried oregano because it has an intense flavour. It is good with tomato. I find that fresh oregano is too pungent.

ROSEMARY: The best time to use fresh rosemary is when you roast potatoes, meat or chicken or grill fish and I use some twigs of rosemary as a brush when I barbecue. I take a bunch of rosemary, make an oil with salt and pepper, then I dip the bunch into the oil and brush the meat and the fish with it.

PARSLEY we use for decoration and to give a fresh flavour to dishes. It is perfect with everything. (This is the reason we say to someone who is everywhere, we say you are like parsley!) It doesn't disturb the flavour and matches most dishes. I also use basil and parsley together in pesto.

BASIL: I always use fresh basil. In the recipe section you will find my personal pesto recipe (page 133) which is, of course, a great expression of basil as is *Ravioli al Pomodoro e Basilico*, my favourite simple dish (page 125).

SAGE: Perfect with any meat or fish. The only recipe that I cook where sage is used on its own is in *Burro e Salvia*, pasta tossed with melted butter, *Parmigiano* and fresh sage. Otherwise I always mix it with rosemary.

THE DIFFERENCE BETWEEN A CAPER AND A CAPERBERRY

A caper is the bud of the caper bush and you'll find it stored in salt or vinegar. If it is left on the bush to turn into a flower, you get a caperberry (see 4) which is larger and is used in *aperitivi*.

So first we have the bud (1), then the flower opens (2), then the flower dies (3) and then the fruit appears (4), the *frutto del cappero* or *cucunci*. Inside the caperberry (4) are seeds which you crunch. In Italy we serve them with Campari and Martini alongside pickled onions.

CAPERS

When you go to Sicily and walk around the islands you find capers everywhere. They just grow wild. These capers are very small and high quality. Whenever you find a small caper that means that the quality is good and they are often stored in salt. The larger ones are stored in vinegar and cost less.

HOW TO USE CAPERS

— You should only use capers in vinegar in salad because if you use them in pasta everything will taste of vinegar.

— When you buy them in salt, wash them well in fresh water and then you can use them for anything.

— If you don't wash them well, you will alter the flavour of the dish. That's especially true when you cook with capers and olives together. Olives are often very salty so when you combine them, your dish could end up inedible.

— You don't need to cut small capers, just leave them whole.

PASTA

We can divide pasta into *pasta fresca* and *pasta secca*, fresh and dried. Fresh pasta is usually made with eggs but sometimes it is made only of flour and water. The traditional egg pasta that you will recognise are *lasagna*, *fettuccine*, *tagliatelle* and *pappardelle*. *Gnocchi* is also a fresh pasta even though it is made of potato. Then we come to stuffed pasta: *ravioli*, *tortellini*, *agnolotti*. I would place *lasagna* and *cannelloni* in this group. Every region has something that is typical.

Pasta is for an Italian what rice is to someone from Asia. Pasta, unlike rice, is never, *ever* a side order. It is always a course on its own. In Italy, the portion is smaller than it is here where it is often served as a main course. In Italy, we serve just 80 to 100 grams of pasta for each person. *Gnocchi* too is always a first course.

In terms of *pasta fresca* or fresh pasta, there is also *acqua e farina* which is made from flour and water. *Strozzapreti* is a good example (it means to 'strangle the priest' because the pasta is formed into a twist). *Orecchiette*, *cavatelli* or *strascinati* are all made from just these two ingredients. *Aqua e farina* pasta takes much longer to cook than egg pasta, about 15-16 minutes.

It is very important to understand why Italians eat their pasta *al dente*. It is so that it is easy to digest – over-cooked pasta is not easy to digest and the texture of pasta *al dente* is far superior. You don't want your pasta soft so that it's like food for babies or old people.

WHY THE SHAPE OF PASTA IS IMPORTANT

The important thing about the shape is that it is linked to the sauce that you need for the pasta. If you have a large amount of sauce, you need something that catches it like *rigatoni* or *penne*. If you have an oily sauce and therefore don't need to use much sauce, it's best to use a long pasta. *Spaghetti* or *linguine* catches less sauce. If you used *penne* instead it would catch lots of dressing and then the pasta would be too oily. Tube pasta like *penne* is used with tomato or creamy sauces. These are simple rules but they work.

HOW TO BUY GOOD PASTA

Good *dried* pasta brands for home cooking are easy to find, for example, De Cecco, Barilla and Buitoni. Good *fresh* pasta is hard to find. In Italy there are shops called *pasta fresca*. They make sheets of *lasagna, gnocchi, ravioli,* whatever you want and you can order in advance if you want something really special. You can colour and flavour pasta with natural ingredients: spinach turns it green, squid ink creates a rich black pasta and you'll even find a red one with *peperoncino* or tomato. If you can find some, try a red pasta with *radicchio*. It is remarkably good.

HOW TO COOK PASTA

To cook pasta you only need boiling water and salt and at least 3 litres of water for pasta for four people. For every litre of water, add 7g of salt. It's not exact, it's a guideline. Don't worry, the salt flavours the pasta and stays in the water so you will not end up eating the salt. Be brave. This is how you make the best pasta. If you don't use salt when you cook the pasta, you will taste only the sauce in the dish whereas you should be able to taste the difference between the sauce and the pasta. So you salt the pasta water and you balance both pasta and sauce.

When you drain the pasta, you must drain it perfectly. If you find that the pasta sauce is too thick, it's better to use the water from the pasta to thin it out. If you are making a pasta dish where the ingredients you are adding are not cooked and where you will have no reason to toss the pasta in the pan, you will need a little hot liquid which comes from the pasta water.

When I cook *rigatoni* with *pecorino* and black pepper, I toss the pasta in the bowl with the cheese and pepper, then add a spoon or two of the water from the pasta to combine it.

FISH, PASTA AND WINE

When I cook fish for pasta, I never use wine because the wine is an added flavour and gives it a different taste. Years ago I was with a chef in Catania in Sicily. He cooked with water instead of wine. I asked him: 'Why do you use only water? Why do you not use wine?'. He said: 'Next time try to cook the same food without wine and you will see the difference'. And I did and I saw the difference ... the wine had been masking the flavour of the fish. It lost its purity of flavour.

Now I only use wine with seabass or brill and only when I cook them in the oven. I always use a good wine whereas most restaurants use cooking wine. Of course, I always use the freshest fish so I don't need to cover up the flavour.

RICE

The varieties of rice that are the most popular in Italy are *arborio, roma, carnaroli, super fino carnaroli and vialone nano*. Rice has become popular all over the country in the last 30 years though it was originally only eaten in the north where it grows in the rice fields of Lombardia. (It's a bit like polenta which was only popular in the north in the past. Now it's everywhere.)

The most important thing we make with rice is *risotto*. It is a dish that takes time and care. I use *arborio* rice because it has enough well-balanced starch to make a creamy *risotto*. Of course you can't make *risotto* with long grain rice because the quantity of starch is very low. What you need in the rice is the starch which makes it creamy and sticks it together.

The procedure to make *risotto* is very easy. You have to *perlare* the rice over a low heat with butter and onion, that is to cook it until it turns the colour of a pearl (but not golden). Then you add hot stock a little at a time (you stop the cooking if you use cold stock and your *risotto* will be soft outside and hard inside). The rice must be just covered with the stock. Then you stir it until the broth is reduced (but not fully absorbed), then you add more stock just covering the rice and stir again. You will see the rice grow in volume, then you add another ladle of stock and so on, until the rice is *al dente*. You need to taste the rice after 15 minutes to make sure the

cooking is going well. You have to pay attention after that. When the rice is *al dente* the rice should be soft outside but with a crunchy bit inside. It has to be a pleasure to eat it. If you feel it is too crunchy you need to cook it a little bit more. The rice will still keep on cooking when you turn the heat off so you need to take that into account.

In another pan, you cook the sauce that you want to use for your *risotto*, then you finish the cooking by combining the cooked rice with the sauce. You can make the sauce earlier if you wish and add it to the hot *risotto* rice. The last thing you do is *mantecare*, that is to add a knob of butter and leave the *risotto* covered in the pan to rest for two or three minutes.
If you are using *Parmigiano*, this is the moment to add it. It takes between 15 to 20 minutes from start to finish to make *risotto*, depending on which rice you use.

Don't make *risotto* if you have to make it for more than 6 people, it is too hard to make for more than this at home. In Lombardia, the chefs tap the plate underneath to distribute the *risotto*, then they turn it upside down to show that it won't spill. You also see lots of television chefs doing this.

Italians are very creative with rice. We use it to make *supplì*, little rice balls which are deep-fried and are often made from leftover *risotto* rice. You can make one stuffed with *mozzarella* which is called *supplì al telefono* — it means '*supplì* on the phone' because when you bite into it, the melting *mozzarella* centre makes a thread of cheese and it looks like a telephone line. In Sicily they make *arancini* from *risotto* rice in the shape of little oranges — because, of course, *arancino* is the Italian word for a small orange.

Another way we eat rice is in *minestra*. We don't eat rice as a side order except in the famous recipe of *Oss Bus* (that's how people from Milan call *Osso Buco*) which is served with saffron *risotto*. When we are sick, we eat *riso in bianco*, rice in butter or olive oil with *Parmigiano*. As a child, if I had flu or a problem with my stomach, this is what my mother gave me.

TOMATOES

I'm sure that tomatoes are one of the great expressions of Italian food around the world. In my cooking I use fresh cherry tomatoes. I buy them on the vine because they don't get crushed and I like the green aroma of the stem.

In Italy we use tinned tomatoes when fresh tomatoes are out of season. It can be hard to find good tinned tomatoes and a lot depends on the variety of tomato that you find in the tin. *San Marzano* tomatoes, for example, are good because the texture and sweetness and acidity are perfectly balanced.

The only way that you can understand a tinned tomato is to take a bowl, turn the tin of tomatoes into it and check the dimensions of the tomatoes. I'm serious! If there are five tomatoes inside, there should be five regular tomatoes, not one small one, then one large one. If they are all of even size, that means that they were picked when they were ripe and not just picked because it suited the producer to pick them at that time.

If the tomatoes are too small then they may not be ripe and there will be a difference in the taste. If you find a white or yellow spot in the tomato, that means the tomato is not ripe. What you have to do before you include a tomato in your cooking is to eat part of it and if it tastes like a

HOW TO FIND A GOOD TINNED TOMATO

– Check the size of the tomatoes in the tin – they should all be the same

size. That means they have been picked at the same stage of ripeness.

The smaller the tomatoes, the less cooking they need.

– The liquid that comes with the tomatoes should not be too thin.

It should look like a *passata*, that is like a thick tomato sauce.

– If you buy a tin of cherry tomatoes and you find one or two unripe ones,

you can use all of them. If there are lots of unripe tomatoes, remove

them as they will ruin the balance of the sauce.

– Tomatoes have more flavour if you cook them with their skins. It should

say it on the tin.

tomato then it is OK to use. If it smells odd, don't use that one but you can use the rest of the tomatoes if they are good.

WHAT VARIETY OF TOMATO SHOULD YOU BUY?

At the moment the Italian tomato industry works with *Roma* tomatoes which are a hybrid of *San Marzano*. The best tinned varieties to buy are *San Marzano*, *Pachino* (which are a cherry tomato), *Collina* (a small and traditional variety of cherry tomato grown on a hill very close to the sea near Sorrento) and *Corbarese* (they are a little rounder than the *San Marzano* which are a long tomato). The difference between *Pachino* and *San Marzano* is in the size: the *Pachino* tomato is like a cherry, round and small and the *San Marzano* is also long but it is meatier. They look different on the plate. The *Pachino* is perfect to serve with fish, on its own or with pasta with fish. It's the best tomato to match with *Vongole* or lobster and it needs very little cooking. In five, six minutes it is cooked. *San Marzano* tomatoes also need very little cooking whereas *Roma* tomatoes need more time, ten to fifteen minutes.

SKIN OR NO SKIN?

There is a great debate between the tinned tomato producers. Some of them want to keep the skin on, others want to peel the tomatoes. Only in Italy could you have this much serious discussion over a tinned tomato! The skin is so important for flavour. For me, it is one of the best parts of the tomato. It is like cooking with prawns – you cook them in the shell because if you peel them you lose flavour. It's the same with tomatoes. It is hard to find tinned tomatoes with the skin on but if you are cooking with fresh tomatoes, try to keep them. Of course you need to ask your guests, especially if you are cooking for children or older people.

When you cook tomatoes for a long time, you will condense the sugar and they should get sweeter. If the tomatoes are not sweet, you can add a little sugar. In Sicily they use sugar even if the tomato is sweet enough. It is not a bad thing to do, it is just a preference. Tomato is a natural food. If you get a crop that is not very sweet, at that stage you need to adjust it. When I work with a tomato I taste it every time I cook it to see if it needs something.

If you use chopped tomatoes, you are in trouble from the start if you don't choose a good brand because the producer can put everything in the tin because you can't see anything. *Passata* is the same. It is hard to find a good one and because the producer knows that you can't see the original tomato, you can find everything in there. There are a few makers of good quality honourable *passata* but you need to try them to find a good one. It's worth paying a little extra.

CURED MEAT

Prosciutto is a general term in Italian for ham. What makes the difference to *prosciutto* is whether it is *crudo* or *cotto* and where it comes from. The mistake that people make is to call all *prosciutto* 'parma ham'. When you ask for parma ham, you are asking for ham from Parma. When you ask for *Prosciutto di Norcia*, you are asking for ham from Norcia.

In Italy we divide ham into *prosciutto crudo* which is the raw one and *prosciutto cotto* which is the cooked one. There are many types of *prosciutto* made in all the regions of Italy. Examples include *San Daniele* or *Bassiano* or something like the one from Abruzzo or *Prosciutto di Montagna* which is usually a little bit more salty than the Parma version. So if you go into a supermarket or cured meat shop called a *Norcineria* in Italy (the name comes from Norcia in Umbria because they were famous for their cured meats) you can find usually six, seven, eight *prosciutto crudo* divided into sweet or salty versions.

There are also the *insaccati* ('*insaccati*' means 'put in a bag or sack', the sack in this case is the skin) which include *salame, mortadella* and *coppa*: they are cured meats that are minced or cut with the knife and put inside a skin and seasoned with herbs and salt and sometimes a little wine. The other kind of cured meat is *non insaccati* which is *prosciutto, speck, bresaola* and *lonza*. These cured meats come from a full part of the animal. You can see what you have immediately when you get a piece of cured meat on the plate. *Non insaccati* are more expensive than *insaccati* because in the *insaccati* you can add cheaper fattier cuts to the good parts of the meat. So *salame* is cheaper than *prosciutto* and *bresaola* is very expensive.

It is important to cut cured meats just before you eat them. If you get a slice of *mortadella* that has been cut two hours before, it looks like it has been sweating in the sun. This is the reason we cut everything to order so it is very fresh and the flavour and colour is completely different. When you go into the supermarket, often the slices look dead.

Many cured meats are made from pork but you find something more special when it is made with wild boar and in north Italy *prosciutto* is also made from venison or other game.

Fresh sausages fall into the *insaccati* category and are popular everywhere in Italy. The most famous of cured meats in Italy is *salame* and it is the most popular. You'll find *Salame di Milano*, *Salame L'Aquila* or the *Ventricina* or the small *Cacciatorino* or the flat one which is typical to Rome called *Schiacciata*.

It's very common to eat cured meat in Italy every day. We use them in the *panini* at lunch. Cured meats are usually included or served on their own in *antipasto* before a full meal. Or you can serve them when you make a

carpaccio with *bresaola* and some rocket salad and *Parmigiano* cheese. Cured meats are full of bad cholesterol and salt so you should be aware of this if you eat them everyday. Another important thing when you prepare the *prosciutto crudo* is that you should leave a border of fat on the meat, that part gives the sweet flavour. The top quality *prosciutto* is the *San Daniele*.

When we match meat with cheese, for sure you also need bread and for a quick meal, it's made as an *antipasto*. I can't remember seeing cured meat being eaten at the end of a meal which is different from cheese which can be used at the end or the beginning. You don't need olive oil with cured meat because there is always fat in it, except for *bresaola* where you need it because it has no fat and otherwise it is too dry.

MARCO CHOOSING CURED MEAT
AT A MARKET IN ITALY

WE FOUND THIS FUNNY LITTLE PIG MADE OF SALAMI IN THE
WINDOW OF A BUTCHER'S SHOP IN PIENZA IN TUSCANY.

CARING FOR YOUR CURED MEATS

– When you buy sliced cured meat, you need to eat it within two days. It's

best to keep cured meat in the fridge wrapped in wax or greaseproof

paper once it is cut. If it is whole, you can keep it for two weeks, no more.

Hang it in a cold kitchen and cut away and discard the top slice each time.

– Don't eat the skin on salami and never give a child a slice of cured meat

with skin because they could choke on it.

– Always buy your cured meats from a trusted supplier like an Italian deli.

Some supermarkets 'kill' cured meats, they even remove the skin

and the fat so they look like a scalped Indian! They leave it in the chilled

section too long. Buy from people who know how to care for them.

HOW TO BUY AND STORE FISH

I am not showing you this picture of a fish because I want to make you scared. I want you to understand what fresh fish, just caught, looks like. Look at the seabass on the left and you will see a few things that are important about understanding when a fish is fresh. The eyes should be bulging. They should not be recessed back into its head. If the eyes are flattened into the head, the fish is not fresh.

The smell of a fish should be a pleasure. Fish should smell of the sea, not of fishiness. The gills, that's the part where the fish breathes, should be red with blood: this means that the fish is absolutely fresh. If there is no blood or if the blood is dark, the fish is over three or four days old or has been defrosted.

How do you store fresh fish? Clean the fish or get your fishmonger to do it for you. Put the fish in a plastic container and keep it in the fridge between one and five degrees. In Italy when we have guests in the house for three days, we say that after that they are like fish and they start to smell! In the restaurant we keep fresh fish for up to two days at the right temperature.

CHEESE

Cheese is important to Italians. We eat it all day from breakfast to after dinner, we cook with it, children take it to school. When I was a child there was always *Parmigiano* or *Grana Padano* and spreadable soft cheese called *Formaggino Mio* in the fridge. Every summer we went to Sicily where my parents were born. We would bring back at least six or seven full wheels of *Pecorino Siciliano* made by a farmer that my father knew. It was something that made me embarrassed because of the smell in the car. I was ashamed to tell my friends that we were bringing back wheels of *pecorino*. Now it's something that I dream of doing and I understand why my father was so happy when he was tasting the cheese. I was saying: 'You're bringing six wheels of *pecorino*. For what!'. When we were together at the table, Papà would say: Look Marco, this is the *pecorino* we brought from Sicily'. People always think that what is made in their part of the country is the best. He was proud to be Sicilian. Now I use cheese a lot in my cooking.

MOZZARELLA is never perfectly round. It has a nodule at the end of it because the maker cuts it off by hand. The word *mozzare* means 'to cut off'. *Caprese*, the salad made with *mozzarella* and tomatoes that is so popular outside of Italy all year round is something that we actually eat especially in the summer when the tomato perfectly matches the *mozzarella* (page 88). It is an *antipasto* that we share rather than eat on our own.

Buffalo *mozzarella* is more expensive than the one made from cow's milk. For everyday dishes we eat cow *mozzarella* because it's half the price of buffalo and it's made everywhere in Italy. It looks the same as buffalo which I prefer because

I think my mother gave me too much cow's *mozzarella* as a child.

HOW TO BUY FRESH MOZZARELLA

Try to find the fresh *mozzarella* that is sold in the bag in its own liquid that has at least ten days shelf life left. It will not be the same as the *mozzarella* we eat in Italy but with it you can make an honourable *Caprese*. Do you ever wonder why buffalo *mozzarella* tastes different outside of Italy? That's because the shelf life of the fresh buffalo *mozzarella* which is made for the export market is about three weeks and in Italy it is less than a week. The problem is that the *mozzarella* is made on Thursday and delivered on Friday to Milan before lunchtime. The truck leaves Milan to arrive here on Tuesday or Wednesday. A few days after it is made, it loses structure and the flavour is completely different. Once you open the bag it is better to use it immediately.

Proper fresh *mozzarella* is like a sponge inside. When you press it, you release a drop of buffalo milk. It is hard to find this outside of Italy. When the *mozzarella* is very soft that means it is going to leave the world! A fresh *mozzarella* feels like an anti-stress ball: it has a tension when you

press it. It rebounds a little.

Cow *mozzarella* is lighter than buffalo which has 25% fat (even though it feels very light). It's hard to cook with buffalo *mozzarella*. At the restaurant, we pass it through a sieve, then leave it to drain in the fridge. By removing the milk, we can use it on pizza (otherwise the pizza would get soggy). If you use too much buffalo *mozzarella*, it takes too long to cook and the middle of the pizza will be raw. When the pizza is almost ready, we take it out, put on the *mozzarella* and cook it for just 20 seconds to melt it.

THE NAME PECORINO COMES FROM PECORA which is the Italian word for 'sheep' and it is, of course, a sheep's cheese. *Pecorino* is produced everywhere in Italy, but the most important producers are in Sardinia where they make *Pecorino Sardo*. *Pecorino Romano* comes from the Lazio area, *Pecorino Toscano* comes from Tuscany and *Pecorino Siciliano* from Sicily.

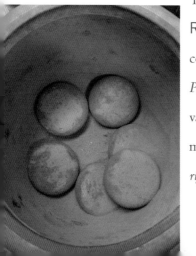

The best selling *pecorino* in Italy is PECORINO ROMANO. We use it in *Campo de' Fiori* for cooking, to grate on top of pasta or mixed with *Parmigiano* or *Grana Padano* for pesto. It is good value for money. The famous *Rigatoni Cacio e Pepe* is made with just *pecorino* and black pepper and *rigatoni*. The original recipe comes from Rome where I am from. They used to take a full wheel which has had the cheese cut out of the middle and they would cook the pasta and toss it inside the wheel, adding only black pepper. In the last 20 years it's not possible to do this because the health authorities say that the cheese can be attacked by bacteria when the hot pasta is added. However, if you know which *trattoria* to go to in Rome, you can still find people making this dish in the old style. At *Campo de' Fiori*, we whisk the *pecorino* into a cream with black pepper and olive oil. We don't toss the pasta in the pan, we do it in the bowl with freshly ground black pepper.

There is also **PECORINO DI FOSSA**. It's an important *pecorino* and it is aged in a pit. *Fossa* means a 'grave' and the cheese is named after it because it is stored three metres underground. It's left for three months and it gets smelly. Even the shape becomes strange when it drains its fat. It's never regular. If you take twenty *Fossa*, they will all be completely different weights and shapes because they are shaped by the elements. This *pecorino* is packed in a vacuum pack inside a sack. It is one of the most expensive *pecorino*.

In Italy we match *pecorino* with fresh fruit and honey and during the Easter period in Rome we eat it with fresh fava beans, just the fresh beans, a piece of *pecorino* and a glass of wine. It's a traditional moment. Some people prefer to drink red, some white. There is even a *pecorino* rhyme:

'*Al contadino non far sapere come è buono il cacio con le pere.*' It means: 'Don't tell the producer how good the *pecorino* is with the pear, otherwise he will eat everything he makes!'. People who eat the cheese say the rhyme at this time of year.

One more thing: the **PECORINO SARDO**. In Sardinia there is an area where the *pastori*, the people that look after the sheep, make a cheese called **CASU MARZU** (*casu* means 'cheese', *marzu* means 'full of mould'). In the past there were literally worms growing in the cheese. The health people banned the cheese but that cheese was more than amazing. It was *buonissimo!* It was a very strong *pecorino*. In Sardinia they continue to produce one you can spread on bread with the same process but without the worms.

Because *pecorino* is a very salty strong cheese, I like it as a table cheese to match with fruit and *mostarda*. I prefer a cheese plate accompanied by a nice glass of wine instead of a sweet dessert. With a nice glass of wine, I can't miss out on a piece of *pecorino*.

FISH AND CHEESE

In Italy, it is something very unusual to mix fish and cheese. A purist would never serve cheese with mussels or clams, it is too strong. But in the Roman seaside, there are a few traditional plates made with *Pecorino Romano*

and lobster or with a different kind of fish. They also stuff ravioli with fish and *Pecorino Romano*. This is something you can find only on the coast of Rome. I cook one dish, either *fettuccine* or *tagliatelle* with seabass or seabream and lemon and *Pecorino Romano*. (see the recipe for *Tagliatelle al Branzino* on page 122). You pan-fry strips of fish with garlic, lemon and add fresh parsley at the end, then you toss it in the pan with the *pecorino*. I don't use any salt because the cheese is salty enough.

A note from the Editor

In Italy you never find a packet of grated *mozzarella*. The *mozzarella* that you often find on pizza in Ireland is a commercial product called cheddar *mozzarella*. It bears no resemblance to real *mozzarella* and costs a lot less. You'll find it on your delivery and convenience pizzas. You also find it grated in bags in the chilled compartments. Marco says please don't use it.

BALSAMIC VINEGAR

Aceto Balsamico di Modena is a general name for balsamic vinegar that is often sold in the supermarket. It can range from a very low quality one which is usually cheaper and can come in a large bottle to a good quality version. However, if you are looking for the best balsamic, the one you should buy is the *Aceto Balsamico di Modena Tradizionale*. It is the aged one made from *Trebbiano* or *Lambrusco* grapes – it must say *Tradizionale Balsamico* on the bottle and come from either Modena or Reggio Emilia to be authentic.

What you find in the supermarket that calls itself balsamic vinegar has no relationship to the real one which has to be older than twelve years to qualify for the title. What you have after 12 years is the *vecchio* and the *ultra vecchio* is 25 years old or more. Our photograph shows a bottle of *tradizionale balsamico* from Modena – you know that because this bottle shape is the only one that can be used for this particular balsamic, by law. They all carry the same label on the top of the bottle.

TRUFFLES

Truffles are mushrooms that live underground and the only way to find them is with the help of a truffle-trained dog or lady pig. There are two varieties of truffle, white (*bianco*) and black (*nero*). The white one is popular in north Italy and is more precious because the consistency and flavour is ten times more intense than the black one. Truffle season begins in summer and lasts until the end of April.

The most important area for the black truffle is Umbria and the main area for the white truffle is Piedmonte. Truffle is not a fundamental ingredient for Italian cooking even if it is an ingredient that can completely transform a dish. You need to be careful when you work with truffle. You can't cook it or you will lose the energy that it brings to your dish. When I make a dish with truffles something magical happens. To cut the truffle you need a shaver, if you cut it with a knife it isn't the same thing. When you shave it you get delicate fine slices so you can use it generously and cover the plate. When you clean the truffle you can't immerse it in water. Use a mushroom brush to remove the soil, wash it briefly in running water and dry it immediately. Keep it in the fridge where it lasts for about a week or ten days at most. Cover it with a little bit of moist kitchen paper so that the truffle thinks it is still in a humid environment. You can store it in a little plastic container with a lid and freeze it for 3-4 months.

COFFEE

In Italy if you are making your breakfast you will have your *espresso* (only we call it *caffè*). An *espresso* is what is made at the bar because it's an express coffee. At home it's made with the *caffettiera* in your house so you can take the time to drink it. You can take a *caffè* any time during the day but four is enough for me.

We drink **ESPRESSO** all day starting from the morning for breakfast, then after lunch and after dinner. Only *espresso*. We don't have a black coffee or americano. For me, it's hard to understand what people are talking about when they ask for a black coffee. For an Italian person a coffee or *caffè* is an *espresso*. Why? Because in the *espresso* there is the best part of the coffee. You have the foam on top which is aromatic and in that short burst of coffee you get all the flavours. In Italy in the morning people stand crowded around and drink espresso and there is not even room to stir it. In Italy you will only find the *espresso* cup or the *cappuccino* cup. In other countries, you find other sizes but in Italy they don't exist.

We drink **LATTE** or **CAPPUCCINO** in the morning with a *cornetto* (like a *croissant*) and we never drink them or a hot chocolate with a meal or after a meal. Never. If you ask for a *cappuccino* after your lunch or your dinner that means you are not Italian, you are a tourist or you have the flu. And if you have flu, you make your *cappuccino* in your own house.

Even the double *espresso* is not Italian. It is something I only discovered when I left Italy (though sometimes when you are drunk your friend will give you two *espresso* to wake you up).

I want to tell you the coffee we have in Italy: *espresso*; *espresso macchiato* (with a little foam of milk); *cappuccino*; *latte macchiato* which is a long glass of milk with a half shot of espresso; *macchiato* which is just *espresso* with a splash or 'stain' of milk and *caffè latte* which is a long glass of hot milk with a full shot of *espresso*. There are a few important brands for coffee: Lavazza, Kimbo, Kosè, Segafredo, Illy. Moak is the main company in Sicily and it is what we use at *Campo de' Fiori*. In my opinion, Moak is one of the best coffees I've ever had. Modica, where it is made is just right beside the village of Rosolini where my parents come from in Sicily, just five minutes drive away.

COFFEE MACHINES

In a professional coffee machine there is a filter cup which holds around 7 grams of coffee. If you overfill it the coffee is pressed too hard and you burn it with the pressure of the water. When you use the *caffettiera* machine which is the coffee machine that every family has in Italy, you can buy the small one for just one cup or a larger one for 15 cups. Before electric coffee machines we only had the *caffettiera*. The system is the same, you put water in the bottom, you have a filter and a container to hold the coffee that bubbles up. If you put too much pressure on the coffee that is a problem because as the boiling water rises, it can burn the coffee. The pressure is strong and there is a valve in the machine to stop the *caffettiera* blowing up. If you speak with my mother or other people they prefer the coffee made at home with the *caffettiera* instead of the coffee made at the bar. It's a ritual. When we finish the lunch we ask: 'Who'll make the coffee?'. If you have five people, which *caffettiera* will I use? If there is only a small *caffettiera* you wait maybe ten or twenty minutes for your coffee. Another thing about the *caffettiera* machine, it should never be washed with washing up liquid, only with water and left to drain.

A coffee machine that works a lot makes a better coffee than a machine that makes a few coffees per day. This is why coffee is never very good in a restaurant with only a few tables. In a busy cafe usually you should get a good coffee because when the machine is hot it makes a better coffee. The machine should be left on all day and overnight if possible.

COFFEE BEANS

There are two main varieties of coffee bean: *robusta and arabica*. *Robusta* gives strength and a good *crema* (Italians judge their *espresso* by whether the sugar can sit on top of the *crema*) while the *arabica* gives flavour and sweetness. There is also a difference between the coffee made in Milan or Sicily and Rome. People in Rome and in the south of Italy prefer a stronger coffee so there is usually more *robusta* in the coffee whereas they prefer more *arabica* in the north.

We also use coffee in desserts. I'm sure that the most famous dessert is *tiramisù* and you know what it means: 'Wake me up'. For me it's a meal with the *mascarpone, savoiardi,* then there is the coffee which is strong, then the sugar and eggs. We eat it after lunch or dinner. It's something that we make for Sunday or for a special occasion. We have the *panna cotta* flavoured with coffee, *affogato al caffè* made with vanilla ice cream and *espresso.*

When I was a child, there were a few places that used to sell pasta and bread and also different kinds of coffee beans. There was a display cabinet divided in parts with the beans and all the mammies, they used to say to the guy behind the counter, give me an ounce of this and an ounce of that and they would grind it. So every family had their own personal blend.

A LITTLE NOTE ON ITALIAN WINE

In Italy grapes grow everywhere. Wine at the beginning of the meal stimulates the appetite so we have the *aperitivo*, like *Prosecco* or another sparkling wine. We celebrate life, birthdays, weddings, the last day of the year with *Prosecco*, *Spumante* or better still the more important *Franciacorta*.

Wine is like an ingredient during a meal so if you decide to go with an *Amarone*, you can't match it with a light pasta or fish dish because you are going to cover the taste of your food. It is better to have fish with white wine and meat with red wine, though you can drink a light red with fish and a strong white with meat. In general, it's better to have a light wine with light food and a more robust wine with stronger food. And it's better to start with light wines and finish with a stronger wine. When you choose the wrong wine, you compromise a meal. What is a wrong wine? It is a wine that you can't match with what you are eating.

FAVOURITE WINES

My favourite grape is *Cabernet Sauvignon*, grown in Italy. My favourite Italian wine is *Brunello di Montalcino* because it's complex and smooth and elegant and fruity and full-bodied and it can last for years and it will become better with time. *Vermentino* from Liguria is a wine you should try because it is minerally, it's fresh, it's even a little bit salty because they have the vineyards near the sea.

COOKING NOTES

PASTA: You need at least 2 litres of water to cook pasta for two people properly and 3 to 5 litres to cook pasta for four people. Pasta needs room to move. At home this amount of water is a lot especially if you have a small kitchen. If you cook pasta often it's worth investing in a *pentola* which is a special pasta pot with a colander insert. It's easier to drain the cooked pasta and you can leave the water to cool before you throw it out. If you don't have a *pentola* then use a large saucepan and have a colander ready at the sink to drain the pasta when it is *al dente*.

AL DENTE is the term used to describe the point that pasta is cooked to so that there is still a 'bite' left. This is critical in the cooking of pasta where over-cooking leads to a collapse in structure and makes it harder to digest. It does not mean that the pasta should be under-cooked. You will usually toss the pasta in the sauce so it will keep on cooking and will be perfect by the time it reaches the table.

GARLIC: For most dishes, I peel the garlic, cut it in half and remove the stem inside as it is hard to digest. I fry the garlic gently in extra virgin olive oil for about two minutes or until it is lightly golden and then discard it when it has done its job of flavouring the oil. I like to fragrance a dish with garlic, not overpower it. The exception is a fish dish where I usually keep the garlic in the dish until the end of cooking.

EXTRA VIRGIN OLIVE OIL: I always use extra virgin olive oil in my recipes. Extra virgin olive oil offers different flavours to a dish depending on what part of Italy it comes from, whether it is young or old, whether it is from one producer or another. It is healthier and as it adds flavour as well as fat, it pays its way. Treat it as if it is another ingredient in the dish.

CAPRESE

Caprese is one of the classic starters of Italian cuisine. In Italy we eat it when it's hot and when we need a fresh, light dish. *Caprese* is more common abroad than in Italy but unfortunately very often in restaurants what is called *Caprese* is just a shadow of the dish we eat in Italy. To get a perfect result, you really need fresh *Mozzarella di Bufala Campana* (a good cow *mozzarella* is also fine), really ripe red tomatoes and fresh basil.

Serves 4

INGREDIENTS
500g of *mozzarella*
4 ripe tomatoes (vine tomatoes are good for this dish)
Salt and freshly ground black pepper (if you like it)
20 small leaves of fresh basil
Extra-virgin olive oil

DIRECTIONS
1. Remove the *mozzarella* from the fridge one hour before serving and leave it sitting in the whey. *Mozzarella* and tomatoes are better when they are served at room temperature. The basil should be stored in cold water with ice cubes to keep it alive and to hold its deep green colour.
2. If you have guests, you could prepare just one shared plate and leave everybody to serve themselves, or you can prepare individual plates. Remove the *mozzarella* from the whey and cut into slices or tear into pieces. Lay on a serving plate. Sprinkle the tomatoes with a pinch of salt and add these and the basil to the plate. Drizzle the dish with a little extra virgin olive oil and, if you wish, some black pepper. Serve some bread on the table to soak up the juices. You can also alternate slices of tomato with *mozzarella* and basil leaves (see our photograph).

MELANZANE GRIGLIATE

You can use this recipe as a starter and serve it with other grilled vegetables, include it in an *Antipasto all'Italiana* with cured meat and cheeses or offer it as a side dish. It is also excellent in a sandwich with ham and cheese. It keeps for up to a week.

Serves 8 as a starter

INGREDIENTS
1kg of aubergines
Salt
2 garlic cloves, peeled, halved and stem removed
Extra virgin olive oil
50g of fresh parsley, finely chopped
Fresh or dry chilli (if you like it)
100ml of vinegar or lemon juice squeezed from 2 lemons

DIRECTIONS
1. Cut the aubergine into slices of 1cm depth or less. Place in a colander and sprinkle with salt. Leave for 30 minutes, rinse, drain and pat dry.
2. Heat the pan over a medium heat (a griddle pan is good). Cook until each slice is chargrilled or lightly golden on both sides.
3. Chop the garlic finely. Oil a dish and layer it with aubergine slices. Sprinkle on parsley, a pinch of salt, garlic and chilli (if you are using it) and drizzle with vinegar or lemon juice. Repeat with each layer, finishing with aubergine.
4. Pour enough olive oil over the aubergine to cover. Leave to marinate for a few hours in the fridge. Remove it an hour before you serve it to allow the oil to come back to room temperature. Serve on a platter with cured meat and cheese.

PROSCIUTTO E MOZZARELLA DI BUFALA

Another Italian cult recipe. All I can say is that good ingredients equal a good plate but with bad ingredients this dish is still better than a McDonald's cheeseburger. A tip about *mozzarella*: always eat it at room temperature because if you take it out of the fridge just before serving, it will lose its flavour.

Serves 4

INGREDIENTS
400g of *mozzarella di bufala*
12 slices of *prosciutto crudo*

DIRECTIONS
1. For presentation, follow your instincts. Cut the *mozzarella* or tear it, fold the *prosciutto crudo* or lay it flat. Do as you wish. A bottle of Chardonnay, preferably from Puglia with a good flavour and fruity characteristics would be a great accompaniment.

ANTIPASTO ALL'ITALIANA

This starter includes cured meats, cheese, grilled vegetables, pickles and olives. It is important that the ingredients have character and are of good quality. In Italy, this dish is often a selection of ingredients that are typical to the area. In Tuscany, you could eat this appetizer with good local ham cut by hand, a little *finocchiona* salame and some *Cacio* cheese from Pienza. In Calabria, you could eat the same dish prepared with *Ventricina* with porcini mushrooms or *pecorino* with chilli. It is not possible to be bored. There are no special preparations unless you decide to use some grilled vegetables. Here are my suggestions...

Serves 4

INGREDIENTS
8 slices of *prosciutto* (you have full freedom to choose which type of *prosciutto* to use, I prefer *San Daniele*)
100g *mortadella* with pistachio
100g *salame* like *Cacciatorino*
100g *Pecorino Sardo* semi-stagionato (*Fiore Sardo* would suit)
100g *Fontina Valdostana* (or any other cheese that is not too salty)
4 artichokes, grilled
100g of mixed olives
A generous basket of fresh bread, sliced

WINE
I would probably go for a red that is not too structured and with good acidity. A good *Chianti* would be the bottle that I would open.

PROSCIUTTO E MELONE

I feel a little bit stupid giving a recipe for this starter as it is so simple, but it's common to find it in some restaurants prepared in a terrible way. The secret, if that is not too grand a word, lies in the two main ingredients: *prosciutto crudo* and melon. The best time for melons is from May to August. The best varieties for this dish (especially in terms of the sweetness that is essential for the *prosciutto crudo*) are *Cantalupo* and *Francesino*. If we cannot find sweet melon we take this dish off the menu. You can use *Prosciutto di Parma* ham or *San Daniele* for the *prosciutto crudo* (which is the name we give to raw cured ham).

Serves 4

INGREDIENTS
12 slices of melon
12 thin slices of *prosciutto*

DIRECTIONS
1. Try to buy the *prosciutto* the day you wish to eat it. Lay down 3 slices of melon on each dish and the same amount of *prosciutto*. That's it!
With this dish, I will drink a good *Verdicchio dei Castelli di Jesi*.

BRESAOLA RUGHETTA E PARMIGIANO

This is a really delicious starter which is light and quick to make. It's important to buy *bresaola* the same day because if you leave it in the fridge for more than one day, the slices will stick to the paper and it will be very difficult to take them off in one-piece.

Serves 4

INGREDIENTS
150g rocket leaves (*rughetta*)
150g *Parmigiano Reggiano* or *Grana Padano* (in one piece)
Extra virgin olive oil
30 slices *bresaola*, cut thinly
Black pepper, freshly ground
1 lemon, cut into quarters

DIRECTIONS
1. Wash the rocket leaves gently and pat dry with paper towel or a clean teatowel.
2. Use a potato peeler to cut the *Parmigiano Reggiano* into thin slices.
3. Divide the rocket leaves between 4 plates and dress with olive oil.
4. Lay the slices of *bresaola* on the rocket leaves. Try to cover the plate but leave a small rim of rocket leaves. Cover the *bresaola* with slices of the *Parmigiano Reggiano.*
5. Add a few grindings of black pepper, drizzle with a little more extra virgin olive oil and add a lemon quarter to each plate.

MINESTRONE

Serves 4

INGREDIENTS
2 courgettes
4 celery sticks
4 carrots, medium
4 potatoes
400g broccoli
1 onion, medium
20ml extra virgin olive oil plus some for dressing the plates
2 vegetable stock cubes
Salt (you may not need it as the stock cubes are salty)
4 button mushrooms, sliced thinly (optional)
Parmigiano Reggiano (optional)

DIRECTIONS
1. Wash the courgette and celery. Peel the carrots and potatoes. Rinse them and cut into small dice. Wash the broccoli and cut the spears off the stem. Discard the stem. Peel the onion and chop finely.
2. Add half the olive oil to a large saucepan. Add the onion, celery and carrot and stir-fry over medium heat for about 5 minutes.
3. Dissolve the stock cubes in 4 litres of boiling water. Pour the hot stock into the saucepan with the vegetables and cook for about 15 minutes.
4. Add the broccoli, potatoes and courgettes and cook for another 10 minutes over medium heat. Check the seasoning. Before serving, add some sliced mushrooms if you wish and cook for 2-3 minutes. Serve in deep bowls. Add a drizzle of extra virgin olive oil and some grated *Parmigiano Reggiano* if you wish.

ZUPPETTA DI PESCE

Serves 2

INGREDIENTS
30ml extra virgin olive oil

1 garlic clove, peeled, halved and stem removed

300g squid or baby squid, cleaned

250g tiger prawns

A pinch of salt

2 pinches of dried oregano

1g dried chilli flakes

300g of tinned cherry tomatoes

10g fresh parsley, chopped

6 leaves of basil

250g cod, cut in 4-6 parts

300g mussels

200g black clams

DIRECTIONS
1. Add 2 tablespoons of olive oil to a large saucepan. Warm it and add the
garlic clove and cook for 2-3 minutes. Add the squid and prawns, a pinch
of salt, the dried oregano and dried chilli flakes and cook for 5-6 minutes
stirring. Add the tomatoes, parsley and the basil and continue to cook for
5 minutes over a medium heat. Add the cod and cook for another 8
minutes. Now add the mussels and the clams.

2. Cover with a lid and continue to cook for another 4 minutes over
a high heat until all the shells are open (discard any that don't open).

3. Take 2 bowls and divide the fish and the sauce between each. Season
with some extra virgin olive oil on top. If you like you can toast some
bread and make a garlic *bruschetta* to serve with this dish.

TORTELLINI IN BRODO

This recipe is very easy, all you have to make is the broth and find good quality fresh *tortellini*. If you are a vegetarian, omit the beef and you have the recipe for a vegetable broth. You can use meat or vegetable *tortellini*.

Serves 4

INGREDIENTS
2 vegetable stock cubes
400g of stewing beef
200g carrots, peeled
160g celery
1 small onion
A pinch of salt
200g of fresh *tortellini*
Extra virgin olive oil
Parmigiano Reggiano, grated

DIRECTIONS
1. Bring 4 litres of water to the boil and add the stock cubes. Heat until dissolved. Cut the beef into 2cm cubes and add to the water with the vegetables. Reduce the heat and simmer the broth for 60-70 minutes. Skim off any white foam. When the meat is tender, remove the vegetables, check the seasoning and add salt if required. If you don't want to use all the broth at once, ladle the amount you need into a clean saucepan and add the *tortellini*. Cook until the *tortellini* are done (just a few minutes) and serve in bowls with a drizzle of olive oil and some grated *Parmigiano Reggiano* on top. You can keep your broth, well covered, for up to 4 days in the fridge. When you want to use it, just reheat what you need in a clean saucepan and add your *tortellini*.

FETTUCCINE AL RAGU'

One of most popular Italian dishes in the world *Ragu'* is often called Bolognese. People from Emilia would be horrified to see how this dish is desecrated by people without respect for our traditions.

Serves 4

INGREDIENTS
2 small carrots
3 celery sticks
1 small onion
4 tbsps extra virgin olive oil
600g of minced meat (400g beef, 100g chicken and 100g pork)
A good grinding of black pepper
A good grating of nutmeg
Salt
200ml of red wine
800g (2 tins) of tomatoes
40g of tomato paste
1 tsp of caster sugar
400g *fettucine* or *tagliatelle*
Parmigiano Reggiano, freshly grated (optional)

DIRECTIONS
1. Finely chop the carrots, celery and onion. Heat the olive oil in a large saucepan. Add the vegetables and fry over gentle heat until soft, stirring continuously until lightly coloured.
2. Turn the heat to medium. Add the meat and cook until the meat is no longer raw. Add black pepper, nutmeg and a pinch of salt.
3. Add the red wine and cook until the wine is absorbed. Add the

tomatoes and tomato paste, another pinch of salt and the sugar. Bring to the boil and reduce to a low heat. Cover, but not completely. Cook for 25-30 minutes, stirring once or twice. Adjust the seasoning. Leave to rest for at least 1 hour and reheat it gently before serving.

4. Cook the *fettuccine* or *tagliatelle* in lots of boiling water (you'll need at least 3 litres of water for four people and 7g of fine salt per litre of water). When it is *al dente*, drain it. Warm the *ragu'* sauce and toss the pasta with the *ragu'*. I love to add some *Parmigiano Reggiano* on top.

A COUPLE OF CLARIFICATIONS:

– 'Spaghetti Bolognese' or 'Bolognaise' or 'Lasagna Bolognese' is not an authentic Italian dish. It doesn't exist in Italy.

– Spaghetti with Bolognese Sauce or with meatballs is something American.

– The best way and the most traditional way to enjoy the *ragu'* is with egg pasta like *tagliatelle*, *fettuccine* or even *pappardelle* but not *spaghetti*. The thicker strands of pasta pick up the correct amount of sauce.

– You don't need to cook your sauce for hours unless you are making a larger quantity.

PENNE DEL DISPERATO

This is a recipe that I began to cook when I was very young. I like to make it very spicy.

Serves 4

INGREDIENTS
250g of *pancetta tesa*
2 garlic cloves, peeled, halved and stem removed
15ml extra virgin olive oil
2 tsps of chilli flakes or 1 spicy fresh red chilli, chopped finely
800g of tinned tomatoes or *passata*
A pinch of salt
160ml of fresh cream
400g of *penne rigate*
50g *Parmigiano Reggiano* or *Grana Padano*, grated
50g *Pecorino Romano*, grated
10g fresh parsley, chopped finely

DIRECTIONS
1. Cut the *pancetta* into little cubes. Fry the garlic gently in olive oil. Add the *pancetta* and fry for 2-3 mins over a low heat. When the *pancetta* is lightly coloured, add the chilli and after a few seconds add the tomato. Add a pinch of salt and simmer for 7-8 minutes over a medium heat.
2. Add the cream and at the same time cook the pasta in boiling water. Usually *penne* takes about 10-13 minutes cooking time depending on the quality. Reduce the sauce until it is thick and cook the pasta until it is *al dente*. When the pasta is ready, drain well and toss it with the sauce. Add both cheeses and the parsley. Toss together and serve.

SPAGHETTI ALLA CARBONARA

It's rare to find *Carbonara* on a restaurant menu in Italy. Maybe in *trattorie* and *osterie* in Rome but a lot less everywhere else. Many Italian chefs like me see *Carbonara* abused, drowned in cream, prepared with chicken, mushrooms, peas, salmon and butter. One thing I have to admit: in Italy there is also a lot of messing about. The recipe I suggest is the one I love.

Serves 4

INGREDIENTS
Salt (7g per litre for the pasta water)
200g of *pancetta tesa* (not the smoked one). Bacon doesn't suit.
400g of *spaghetti*
Extra virgin olive oil
4 egg yolks and 2 whites
80g of grated *Parmigiano Reggiano*
80g of grated *Pecorino Romano*
Black pepper, freshly ground

DIRECTIONS
1. Boil the water for the pasta and add 7g of salt for each litre.
2. Remove the rind from the *pancetta* with a sharp knife and cut it into small chunks. When the water is boiling, add the *spaghetti*.
3. Add a little olive oil to a pan and fry the *pancetta* until it is crispy.
4. In a generous bowl mix the egg yolks and egg whites with the *Parmigiano*, *Pecorino Romano* and a generous amount of black pepper.
5. Drain the pasta and add it to the bowl with the egg mixture immediately. Add the *pancetta* and the liquid that is in the pan. Stir gently without breaking the *spaghetti*. Serve as soon as possible and eat it when it still hot. If you wait too long it will become sticky.

LINGUINE AI FRUTTI DI MARE

Serves 4

320g prawns
400g squid
400g mussels
300g clams
Salt (7g for the pasta boiling water and a pinch for the sauce)
Extra virgin olive oil
2 garlic cloves, peeled, cut in half and stem removed
Dried chilli, to taste
10g of chopped fresh parsley
250g tinned cherry tomatoes
Freshly ground black pepper
400g *linguine*

1. Clean and rinse the fish in fresh water. Wash the prawns and remove
the black thread inside. Cut the squid into medium-sized strips. Clean the
mussels and clams removing any grit and throw away any that are open.
2. Boil the water for the pasta and add the salt.
3. Add olive oil to a large saucepan or frying pan with a lid. Add the garlic
and fry over gentle heat. Add the prawns, squid, a pinch of salt, dried
chilli and half the parsley and stir-fry for a minute over medium heat.
Add the cherry tomatoes and a few grindings of black pepper. Cook for
7-8 minutes stirring continuously over a low heat.
4. Meanwhile cook the pasta *al dente* so it will be ready.
5. Add the mussels and clams to the pan with the other fish, turn the heat
to high, put the lid on and cook until they open. Drain the pasta when it is
al dente and toss it in the sauce in the pan. Pour a little extra virgin olive
oil over the pasta and sprinkle on some parsley.

FARFALLE AL SALMONE

Serves 4

INGREDIENTS
2 tbsps extra virgin olive oil
2 garlic cloves, peeled, halved and stem removed
280g smoked salmon, cut into strips
200ml fresh cream
15g of fresh parsley, chopped
1 tbsp of tomato *passata* or 1 tsp of tomato paste
Freshly ground black pepper
400g of *farfalle* (or you can use *penne*)
Salt (7g per litre for the pasta boiling water plus 1 teaspoon for the sauce)

DIRECTIONS
1. Put the extra virgin olive oil in a frying pan and warm it for about 30 seconds. Fry the garlic until it becomes golden (about 2 minutes), then remove and discard it.
2. Add the smoked salmon and cook for 1 minute over a low heat, turning the salmon gently once to let it catch the heat. Add the cream, ⅔ of the parsley, the tomato *passata* or paste (it gives the sauce a lovely pink colour) and a good grinding of fresh black pepper. Cook it over a gentle heat for 3 to 4 minutes until the sauce thickens.
3. In the meantime, bring the water to the boil in a large saucepan and when the water has boiled, add the salt and the *farfalle* (or *penne*) to the water. Cook the pasta until it is *al dente* (between 9-12 minutes). Drain the pasta well and add to the pan with the salmon and toss it with the sauce for less than a minute. Finish the dish with a drop of extra virgin olive oil and garnish the plates with the remaining parsley.

FETTUCCINE GAMBERI E ZUCCHINE

Serves 4

INGREDIENTS
20 tiger prawns on the shell with no heads
4 small fresh cherry tomatoes
5 tbsps of extra virgin olive oil
2 garlic cloves, peeled, halved and stem removed
Salt (7g per litre of pasta boiling water and 1 tsp of salt for the sauce)
Black pepper, freshly ground
20g fresh chopped parsley
300g courgettes, cut into batons
400g *fettuccine*

DIRECTIONS
1. Cut the prawns in half, leaving them on the shell. Cut the cherry
tomato into quarters. Take a frying pan and warm 3 tablespoons of olive
oil over a low heat for less than a minute. Fry the garlic until golden,
then remove and discard it. Turn the heat to medium and add the
prawns. Add a pinch of salt and two grindings of black pepper. After 2
minutes turn the prawns and add the cherry tomatoes, ⅔ of the parsley
and the courgettes. Leave the sauce to cook for 4 to 5 minutes until the
courgettes become softer. Taste and adjust the seasoning.
2. In the meantime bring the water to the boil, add the salt (7g per litre)
and *fettuccine* and cook until *al dente*. Drain the pasta and toss with the
prawns and courgettes. Finish each plate with a drizzle of olive oil and
garnish plates with the remaining fresh chopped parsley.

TAGLIATELLE AL BRANZINO

This recipe was borrowed from a colleague from Anzio (thank you Vitto).
It's the encounter of fish with cheese which is very typical on the coast
near Rome.

Serves 4

INGREDIENTS
4 tbsps of extra virgin olive oil
1 garlic clove, peeled, halved and stem removed
600g of sea bass fillets with no skin or bones and cut into strips
A beautiful bunch of parsley, chopped finely
1 lemon, juice and peel (chop the peel finely)
400g of egg pasta, *tagliatelle* or *tonnarelli*
Salt (7g per litre of pasta water and a pinch for the fish)
150g *Pecorino Romano*, grated
Freshly ground black pepper

DIRECTIONS
1. Bring the water to boil in a large saucepan. Add 2 tablespoons of oil to
a large non-stick pan and fry the garlic over a medium heat until golden.
Remove and discard. Add the seabass strips to the pan with a pinch of
salt, half the parsley and the lemon juice and cook over medium heat for
3-4 minutes.
2. In the meantime cook the pasta. Drain the pasta when it is *al dente* and
add to the pan. Add 2 tablespoons of olive oil and the *Pecorino Romano*.
3. Toss for a few seconds until the cheese is melted. Finish each dish
with the lemon peel, black pepper and the rest of the chopped parsley.

SPAGHETTI ALLA PUTTANESCA

Serves 4

INGREDIENTS
5 tbsps of extra virgin olive oil
1 garlic clove, peeled, halved and stem removed
60g pitted black olives, sliced finely
20g capers in salt, rinsed and roughly chopped (about 30 capers)
400g (1 tin) of tomatoes
3 tbsps of fresh parsley, chopped finely
1 tsp of dried oregano
1 small dried chilli, chopped finely or ½ tsp of chilli flakes
Salt (7g per litre for the pasta boiling water plus a good pinch
for the sauce)
1 small pinch of caster sugar (if the tomatoes are not sweet)
400g *spaghetti*
Freshly grated *Parmigiano Reggiano* or *Grana Padano* (optional)

DIRECTIONS
1. Put 3 tablespoons of extra virgin olive oil in a frying pan and warm it.
2. Add the garlic and fry until it turns golden (about 2 minutes), then
remove and discard it. Add the black olives, capers, tomatoes, two
tablespoons of parsley, the dried oregano, chilli, a pinch of salt and a
small pinch of caster sugar if you are using it. Cook the sauce over a
medium heat for 10-12 mins until the sauce thickens.
3. Bring water to the boil in a large saucepan and add 7g of salt per litre
of water. Add the *spaghetti* and cook until the pasta is *al dente* (between
9-12 minutes). Drain the pasta, add to the frying pan with the sauce and
toss before serving on hot plates. Finish with olive oil, the rest of the
parsley and a grating of *Parmigiano Reggiano* if you are using it.

RAVIOLI AL POMODORO E BASILICO

This recipe can be made with every type of stuffed *ravioli*. Use the fresh one that you find in the chilled section of any good deli or supermarket. We don't use onions because we want the tomatoes and basil to shine.

Serves 4

INGREDIENTS
5 tbsps extra virgin olive oil
600g tinned cherry tomatoes
Salt (7g per litre for the pasta boiling water plus a pinch for the sauce)
1 pinch of caster sugar (if the tomatoes are not sweet)
30 leaves basil with stalks, washed, dried (reserve 4 leaves for garnish)
500g fresh *ravioli* filled with *ricotta* cheese and spinach
Parmigiano Reggiano, grated

DIRECTIONS
1. Put 5 tablespoons of extra virgin olive oil in a frying pan and warm over medium heat for a minute. Add the tomatoes, a good pinch of salt, a pinch of sugar if required and the basil with stalks. Leave the sauce to cook for 10 to 12 minutes until it thickens. Remove the stalks from the basil and discard (the stalks will have enhanced the flavour of the dish but they don't look good on the plate).
2. In the meantime bring the water to the boil, add the salt and the *ravioli* and leave them to cook in the boiling water until they are *al dente* – you will find instructions on the packet. Drain the pasta well in a colander, add to the frying pan and toss gently with the sauce for less than a minute. Serve on warm plates and finish with a drizzle of extra virgin olive oil. Garnish the plates with a leaf of fresh basil and *Parmigiano Reggiano*.

FETTUCCINE AI FUNGHI

Serves 4

INGREDIENTS
5 tbsps extra virgin olive oil
1 garlic clove, peeled, halved and stem removed
500g button mushrooms (wiped clean and cut into thin slices)
Salt (7g per litre for the pasta water plus a pinch for the sauce)
Nutmeg, grated (about ¼ of a teaspoon)
3 tbsps chopped fresh parsley
Black pepper, freshly ground
400g egg fettuccine
4 tbsps of grated *Parmigiano Reggiano*

DIRECTIONS
1. Warm 3 tablespoons of extra virgin olive oil in a frying pan.
2. Add the garlic to the pan and fry gently until it is golden (about 2 minutes). Remove the garlic and discard.
3. Add the mushrooms and cook over a high heat until they release their water. They will take about 3 minutes to cook. Add a pinch of salt, the nutmeg, two tablespoons of parsley and the black pepper and continue cooking until the water from the mushrooms has completely evaporated.
4. Bring the water to the boil for the pasta. Add the salt and *fettuccine*. Cook until *al dente* (between 5-7 minutes). Drain well in a colander.
5. Add the cooked pasta to the pan with the mushrooms and add the last 2 tablespoons of extra virgin olive oil and half of the grated *Parmigiano Reggiano*. Toss everything together for about half a minute. Serve the pasta in a large warmed bowl or in individual plates, sprinkling with the rest of the cheese and decorate with the remaining chopped parsley.

PENNE ALL'ARRABBIATA

Serves 4

INGREDIENTS
5 tbsps of extra virgin olive oil
2 garlic cloves, peeled, halved and stem removed
400g (1 tin) of tinned tomatoes
Salt (7g per litre of pasta boiling water plus 1 teaspoon of salt for
the sauce)
3 tbsps of fresh chopped parsley
2 dried chillies or 1 teaspoon of chilli flakes
1 pinch of caster sugar, if the tomatoes are not sweet
400g *penne*

DIRECTIONS
1. Put 3 tablespoons of extra virgin olive oil in a frying pan and warm it
over a low heat for less than a minute. Add the garlic and fry until it
turns golden, then remove and discard it.
2. Add the tomatoes, breaking them up with a wooden spoon.
Add 1 teaspoon of salt, two tablespoons of parsley, the dried chilli or
chilli flakes and a little pinch of caster sugar if needed.
Let the sauce cook over medium heat for 10-12 minutes until the sauce
thickens. You need to watch it to make sure it doesn't dry out.
3. In the meantime boil the pasta water. Add salt to the water. Add the
penne. Cook until it is *al dente*. Drain the pasta well.
4. Add the pasta to the frying pan with the sauce, add 2 tablespoons of
extra virgin olive oil and mix everything together for about half a minute.
Serve the *penne* with the sauce on the plates and decorate using the
remaining fresh chopped parsley.

SPAGHETTI AL FUOCO

'Fuoco' means 'at the fire' so this dish has to be spicy. You need to find the ripest, juiciest tomatoes. It's important that you cut each cherry tomato into 8 pieces so they are the right size for this dish.

Serves 4

INGREDIENTS
500g ripe cherry tomatoes
20 leaves of basil, torn
100g *ricotta infornata* – reserve some to finish each plate
100g *Pecorino Romano*, grated
1 teaspoon of chilli flakes
30g of fresh parsley, chopped finely
1 tsp of dried oregano
150ml extra virgin olive oil
A good grinding of black pepper
½ tsp of caster sugar
Salt (7g for each litre of pasta boiling water plus a pinch for the sauce)
400g *spaghetti*

DIRECTIONS
1. Cut each cherry tomato into quarters, and cut each quarter in half again. Mix with the rest of the ingredients except the *spaghetti* (leave some *ricotta* aside to put on top of the dish). Leave to marinate for 20 minutes at room temperature.
2. Bring the water to the boil in a large saucepan, add the salt and the pasta and cook until *al dente* (between 9-12 minutes). Drain the pasta well and add to the bowl with all the ingredients and toss. Top each dish with some *ricotta* and a drizzle of olive oil.

LINGUINE AL PESTO

Here's my personal pesto recipe. Store pesto in the fridge for 2-3 days. Just add a little more oil to cover it. Remove it one hour before use.

Serves 4

INGREDIENTS
50g basil, leaves only
A pinch of salt
150ml of extra virgin olive oil
40g of pinenuts
20g of walnuts
½ garlic clove, peeled, halved and stem removed
20g *Parmigiano Reggiano*
20g *Pecorino Romano*
400g *linguine*
Salt (7g for each litre of pasta boiling water)

DIRECTIONS
1. Make the pesto by hand or in a food processor. If you go with the mortar and pestle, put in all the basil with the salt and ⅓ of the olive oil. Pound until you get a soft green paste. Add pinenuts, walnuts and garlic and another ⅓ of oil. Pound until all the nuts and the garlic are blended. Put the green paste in a bowl and add the cheese. Mix with a spoon adding the rest of the oil. If you use a food processor blend all the ingredients together except the cheese. Pulse for a few seconds, then pulse until all the ingredients are reduced to a paste. Put the pesto in a bowl and add the cheese. Stir with a spoon. Bring the water to the boil in a large saucepan. Add the salt and pasta. Cook until *al dente*. Drain. Toss the pasta in a bowl with the pesto (never heat the pesto).

CARNE

COSTOLETTE DI AGNELLO AL VINO BIANCO

You may think that this recipe is too simple to be good. But simple things are very often the best. Ask your butcher for the best lamb – Spring lamb is good. You can eat this dish with your hands and believe me, it is not a sin to do this. It's a pleasure.

Serves 4

INGREDIENTS
12 lamb cutlets
2 tbsps of extra virgin olive oil
A knob of butter
1 garlic clove, peeled, halved and stem removed
5g of fresh rosemary leaves
5g of fresh sage leaves
A pinch of fine salt
A good grinding of black pepper
100ml of dry white wine

DIRECTIONS
1. Warm a large non-stick pan and place your cutlets in it, making sure there is plenty of space for each one (you don't need any oil). Cook the lamb for 6-7 minutes on each side over a medium heat.
2. While the lamb is cooking, warm the olive oil and butter in a saucepan. Add the garlic, rosemary, sage, salt and pepper. Add the wine and cook over a medium heat until reduced by half. Pour the wine sauce into the pan with the lamb. Cook over a low heat for a minute, turning the cutlets in the sauce until all of them are dressed. Serve immediately.

BISTECCA ALLA FIORENTINA

This is the most famous meat dish made in Tuscany. There are just a few rules to follow. Choose the best T-bone steak that you can. You'll need between 500g to 1kg for 2 people, depending on how hungry you are. Don't use any oil on the meat before you cook it because the heat will burn the oil. Place the steak on a hot griddle or frying pan or barbecue and leave it for a few minutes until it sears before you turn it.

Serves 2

INGREDIENTS
2 T-bone steaks between 500g-1kg
Salt (Maldon is good)
Black pepper, freshly ground
A nice quality of extra virgin olive oil
Lemon quarters (optional)

DIRECTIONS
1. Cook your steak for 3-4 minutes per side in a very hot pan, without oil, if you want it rare and 6-7 minutes per side for medium. Serve on a large plate and finish with a pinch of salt, a generous amount of extra virgin olive oil and black pepper and offer lemon quarters on the side. I like to squeeze the juice on the steak. I would suggest not to overcook the meat in order to enjoy your *Fiorentina* at its best.

BISTECCA CON SALSA AL PEPE VERDE

Serves 2

INGREDIENTS
2 tbsps extra virgin olive oil
50g green peppercorns in brine, drained
30ml dry white wine
A pinch of salt
200ml of fresh cream
2 sirloin steaks each weighing about 350-400g each if they are on the
bone or 250-300g each off the bone

DIRECTIONS
1. Take a large frying pan and add the olive oil. Add the green
peppercorns and when they start to fry, crush them with any utensil you
have. I use a wooden pestle. Leave to gently fry for 20 seconds and add
the white wine and the salt. Reduce the wine to half and add the cream.
Cook for a few minutes until the sauce is thick. Keep warm or reheat
when your steaks are done.
2. Take a large frying pan or skillet, preferably made of cast-iron.
Heat it until you can barely hold your hand over it (don't add any oil).
Add the steaks. Leave the steaks to cook and seal on one side so the
flesh doesn't tear when you lift it, then turn it over. Cook it to your
liking. I like it done for 3-4 minutes per side. Season the meat with salt
and leave to rest for 5 minutes. Serve with the hot green peppercorn
sauce on the side.

BOCCONE DELL' APPUNTATO

Serves 4

INGREDIENTS
4 chicken breasts, free-range if possible
100g boiled spinach, squeezed dry
100g of smoked *Scamorza* cheese, cut into four slices
Salt, a pinch and freshly ground black pepper
Butter
400g mushrooms, cleaned (button are fine)
2 garlic cloves, peeled, halved and stem removed
Nutmeg, two pinches
400ml single cream
Parsley, chopped for garnish

DIRECTIONS
1. Butterfly the chicken breasts using a sharp knife. Place your hand on
the breast. Cut along the edge moving towards the center. Don't cut all
the way through. Fill the breasts with spinach, *Scamorza*, a sprinkling of
salt and a grinding of black pepper. Close the top flap over the breast to
close. Lay them in a large pan with a knob of butter, cover with tin foil
and bake at 200°C/400°F/Gas Mark 6 for 30-35 minutes or until the
juices of the chicken run clear when cut with a knife.
2. Make the sauce. Oil a large pan and fry the garlic over gentle heat
until golden. Remove and discard. Add the mushrooms and cook over
high heat for 2-3 mins. Add salt, nutmeg and black pepper. Cover the pan
with a lid and cook the mushrooms over medium heat. When the liquid
evaporates, add the cream and reduce. Serve the chicken covered with
mushroom sauce. Finish with chopped parsley.

POLLO ARROSTO

This dish used to be one of the favourite second courses in my family when I was a child. This recipe is good, simple, healthy and cheap and the best side order to match with it is roast potatoes. It is a good way of showing how we used dried herbs in Italian cooking. You can use a whole chicken if you wish but adjust the cooking times to suit. If you are using a whole chicken, make sure to massage the inside with the honey mixture.

Serves 4

INGREDIENTS
1 teaspoon of honey
The juice of ½ lemon
2 teaspoons of dried rosemary
3 sprigs of fresh rosemary, leaves only
A good pinch of salt
A good grinding of black pepper
4 chicken legs
4 garlic cloves
Extra virgin olive oil

DIRECTIONS
1. Preheat the oven to 200°C/400°F/Gas Mark 6.
2. Mix the honey, lemon, dried rosemary, fresh rosemary leaves, salt and black pepper together. Massage the chicken legs with the mixture on both sides.
3. Put the chicken legs in an oven dish with the garlic.
4. Bake the chicken for 45-55 minutes until the chicken is golden and the juices run clear.

TAGLIATA DI FILETTO ALL'ACETO BALSAMICO

A fantastic recipe. Make sure to get the best and tender meat that you can.
The high quality of the ingredients will make the difference.

Serves 2

INGREDIENTS
100g *Parmigiano Reggiano* or *Grana Padano* (in one piece)
2 nice sirloin steaks (250g each)
A few drops of *Aceto Balsamico di Modena* or *Reggio Emilia*
100g rocket leaves, washed and patted dry
Salt
A nice extra virgin olive oil

DIRECTIONS
1. Cut the cheese with a potato peeler into thin shards.
2. Cook your sirloin as you prefer (3 or 4 minutes for each side to get it
rare or 6 to 7 minutes to get it medium. If you want to cook it for more
time then I'm not responsible for your sins).
3. When the meat is ready, put some rocket leaves on each plate. Cut the
steak with a sharp knife on the diagonal into 2-3cm slices. Lay the meat
on the rocket leaves, season with salt, a few drops of balsamic vinegar,
cover with the shards of cheese and finish with extra virgin olive oil.

AGNELLO DEL PARADISO

This is a personal recipe that I like for the intensity of the flavours. Choose very nice cutlets of lamb that are not too fatty. Spring lamb is ideal.

Serves 4

INGREDIENTS
12 lamb cutlets
A pinch of fine salt
Freshly ground black pepper
12 slices of *pancetta tesa* (smoked is not good)
200ml of red wine
200g of black olives (*Tipo Gaeta* or *Leccino*)
4 garlic cloves, peeled

DIRECTIONS
1. Season the lamb with salt and black pepper.
2. Wrap each of the lamb cutlets with a slice of *pancetta*.
3. Place the wrapped cutlets in a large oven-proof dish. Pour the wine over the lamb. Add the olives and garlic. Leave to marinate for at least two hours.
4. Preheat the oven to 220ºC/425ºF/Gas Mark 7. Cover the lamb dish with aluminium foil and place in the oven. Bake for 40 minutes. Turn the oven off. Remove the foil and pour the liquid that is left in the dish into a saucepan. Put the foil back on the lamb and return to the oven to keep warm. Reduce the juices from the lamb over a medium heat in a small saucepan until thick.
5. Divide the lamb between plates, top with sauce and some olives.

MARCO IN DISCUSSION WITH A LADY SHOPPER AT THE MARKET AT VINCI IN
ITALY. SHE HAS CHOSEN SWORDFISH FOR LUNCH AND IS GOING HOME TO
COOK IT IN A SPLASH OF WHITE WINE.

IMPEPATA DI COZZE

Everything about this dish will depend on the freshness and quality of the mussels. If your saucepan is not big enough to contain all the mussels, cook them in two batches or reduce the quantity. One kilo per person is the right amount to make a nice portion. Mussels should be cooked just until they open. If you over-cook them you will make them rubbery and unpleasant to eat.

Serves 4

INGREDIENTS
Extra virgin olive oil
2 garlic cloves, peeled
4kg of mussels, cleaned
30g fresh parsley, chopped
A generous amount of black pepper, freshly ground
2 lemons, cut in quarters

DIRECTIONS
1. You will need a pan or a pot with a lid that is large enough to comfortably contain the mussels. Turn the heat to medium and add extra virgin olive oil and the garlic.
2. Add the mussels, half of the parsley and a half ladle of water. Turn the heat to high, cover with the lid and cook for a few minutes, just until the mussels are all open, shaking the pan as you go. Discard any mussels that stay closed. Add a few grindings of black pepper.
3. Serve the mussels in soup bowls with some of the cooking liquid, a splash of oil and a lemon quarter. Bring some spoons to the table – you will need them. It's also important to bring a big dish to the table for the empty shells.

CAPESANTE AL BRANDY

This dish of scallops and tiger prawns in a brandy and cream sauce is one of my signature dishes. It is one of the few recipes where I use cream.

Serves 2 (doubles easily)

INGREDIENTS
3 tbsps of extra virgin olive oil
1 garlic clove, peeled, halved and stem removed
10 tiger prawns on the shell
10 fresh scallops
A pinch of salt
2 tbsps of brandy
6 tbsps of fresh cream

DIRECTIONS
1. Warm the extra virgin olive oil in a non-stick frying pan over a medium heat. Add the garlic and cook until lightly golden. Add the tiger prawns. Stir until they change colour to pink. Add the scallops and continue to cook over a medium heat for 4 minutes, turning the scallops once – be gentle so you don't break the scallops.
2. Reduce the heat to low. Sprinkle on the salt and add the brandy and the cream. Avoid flaming the brandy by keeping the pan over the heat. Continue cooking until the cream is thick which will take between 4 to 5 minutes. Be careful not to caramelise the sauce too much or to burn the cream. Serve immediately.

CALAMARETTI AL SUGO

You can make this dish as both a starter or a main course. You will find baby squid at any good fish shop – ask the fishmonger to clean them for you. You can use the tentacles if you wish. (I wish!)

Serves 4

INGREDIENTS
1kg of baby squid
3 tbsps of extra virgin olive oil plus some to dress the plates
2 garlic cloves, peeled
A pinch of salt
1 small fresh chilli or ½ tsp of chilli flakes
400g of tinned cherry tomatoes
1 teaspoon of dried oregano
30g of fresh parsley, chopped finely

DIRECTIONS
1. Rinse the squid and cut it into one inch strips. If you are using the tentacles, leave them whole.
2. Add extra virgin olive oil to a large pan and add the garlic. Fry for a minute, then add the squid and stir. Cook for another minute, then add the salt, chilli and 2 tbsps of water. Cook for 3-4 minutes over medium heat. Add the tomatoes and dried oregano and finish cooking until you have a thick sauce. Serve dressed with some extra virgin olive oil and fresh parsley.

GAMBERI ALLO ZAFFERANO

Choose your prawns carefully. Ask the fishmonger to keep the heads but peel the prawns and leave the end of the tail attached. This will add flavour and make it easier to eat as you can pick up the prawn by the tail. You can make this dish successfully with frozen prawns.

Serves 4

INGREDIENTS
A knob of butter
1 garlic clove, peeled, halved and stem removed
20 prawns (defrosted if frozen)
A pinch of salt
100ml of dry white wine
A pinch of saffron

DIRECTIONS
1. Melt the butter over a medium heat and add the garlic. When it is lightly golden, add the prawns and fry them for 3 minutes making sure not to brown the butter.
2. Turn the prawns in the pan. Season them with salt and add the wine and the saffron. Stir the saffron with the wine and the butter until everything turns golden. Leave the wine to reduce and serve the prawns with sauce immediately.

SPAGHETTI CON LE VONGOLE

A classic, for me. It's a recipe from my region and ideal for people who love pasta with fish. I like to serve the clams with their shells so it's very important that you check the clams one by one and remove any sand.

Serves 4

INGREDIENTS
400g *spaghetti*
Salt
Extra virgin olive oil
2 garlic cloves, peeled, halved and stem removed
Dried chilli
100g tinned cherry tomatoes
1kg clams (*Palourde* are good)
10g chopped fresh parsley

DIRECTIONS
1. Boil the water for the pasta and add 7g of salt for each litre. Add the pasta and cook until *al dente*.
2. Meanwhile add olive oil to a large frying pan, add the garlic, dried chilli and the cherry tomatoes and cook for 3-4 minutes over a medium heat.
3. Add the clams to the sauce with a tablespoon of your boiling pasta water. Cover with a lid and cook over high heat for 4-5 minutes until all the shells are open. Remove from heat, drain the pasta and toss with the sauce and the chopped parsley. Serve immediately. Do not forget to bring an empty bowl to the table for the shells.

INSALATA DI MARE

This is a dish to make when you have time. Whenever I prepare it, I keep tasting it as I go. Fresh fish is best but frozen works too. You need to adjust the dressing each time you make it to match the fish you choose.

Serves 4

INGREDIENTS
400g squid
400g octopus
400g prawns
1kg mussels
1kg clams
Juice of 2 lemons
4 tsps of white wine vinegar
150g celery
150g carrots
A beautiful bunch of parsley, chopped finely
200g of olives with stones (*Gaeta* or *Leccino*)
Extra virgin olive oil
Salt and freshly ground black pepper

DIRECTIONS
1. Ask your fishmonger to clean the squid and octopus. If the prawns are really fresh, I shell them and marinate them in lemon juice. Otherwise boil them for a few minutes and then shell them.
2. Clean the mussels, put them in a pan with a few tablespoons of water over a high heat with a lid and wait a few minutes for them to open. Remove from the pan and leave them to cool (discard any that do not open). Do the same with the clams using another pan and fresh water.

3. Octopus and squid need to be boiled in salty water for at least 40 minutes. Remember that if the octopus is large it will take longer than the squid so put the squid in a few minutes later.

4. When all the ingredients are ready (cooked and cold), put them together in one bowl with the lemon and vinegar. Leave everything in the fridge to marinate for at least 2 hours.

5. Clean and cut the celery and carrots into small pieces.

6. Remove the fish from the fridge and drain any liquid that has leached out. Add the vegetables, parsley and olives and dress with a generous amount of extra virgin olive oil.

7. Now it's the moment for a little taste. Season the fish with salt and black pepper. Serve this dish at room temperature (leave it out of the fridge for an hour).

A NOTE FROM MARCO

– Do not use black olives without stones, they taste terrible.

– Never serve it hot – it's a salad.

– Do not use mayonnaise or you will risk hell!

– Do not use extra virgin olive oil of a low quality. It's better to use a soft and fruity olive oil from the south of Italy.

– Do not throw away any leftovers – they will be good for the next day, sometimes even better.

TONNO ALLA LIVORNESE

A few tips! You need to use very fresh tuna. Make sure the tuna is not taken from the end of the loin, otherwise it will be full of nerves. Don't even think about using capers in vinegar or you will destroy the dish.

Serves 2

60g black olives with stones (*Gaeta*, *Leccino* or *Kalamata*)
4 tbsps extra virgin olive oil
½ small onion, chopped finely
1 garlic clove, peeled, halved and stem removed
15g of capers (in salt), rinsed well
200g of tinned cherry tomatoes (½ a tin)
A good pinch of salt
A pinch of caster sugar to taste
½ teaspoon of dried oregano
2 tuna loin, 200g each

INGREDIENTS
1. Remove the stones from the olives. Warm 2 tablespoons of olive oil in a saucepan and add the onion and the garlic and fry for 3 minutes. Remove the garlic when golden and add the capers and the olives. Fry for one more minute and add the tomato. Season with the salt, sugar and dried oregano. Bring the sauce to the boil, then reduce to a low heat. Cook for 15 minutes until the sauce is thick. Oil the tuna with a few drops of olive oil. Warm a non-stick frying pan and add the tuna. Cook until it is done to your taste. I leave it rare in the centre so that's 2-3 minutes for each side depending on the thickness of your fish. Serve the tuna with sauce and dress with olive oil.

ORATA IN PADELLA

Is it possible to prepare a whole fish in a frying pan? Of course it is. My advice is to cook it for just 2 people – the real problem is the pan which needs to be big enough. You'll need a lid too.

Serves 2

INGREDIENTS
2 whole sea bream, 300-400g each, cleaned
2 sprigs of rosemary
2 sprigs of sage
2 garlic cloves, peeled, halved and stem removed
Salt
Extra virgin olive oil
1 lemon, cut in half
Fresh black pepper
Parsley, fresh to garnish

DIRECTIONS
1. Take a large non-stick pan that is big enough to contain both fish. Divide the herbs and garlic between the fish and stuff them with it. Sprinkle on some salt. Add extra virgin olive oil to the pan and place it over a medium heat. Put the fish in the pan and cover with a lid, tilting it to the side so that the fish fries and doesn't stew. If you hear the pan making strange noises, don't panic. Cook the fish for 10-12 minutes and gently turn the fish, using two forks or a palette knife (don't puncture the fish or you will dry it out). Cook the fish on the other side for another 10-12 minutes. When the fish is cooked serve it on a plate with the head. Bring extra virgin olive oil, salt, the lemon, black pepper and parsley to the table.

PATATE AL FORNO

Serves 4

INGREDIENTS
1kg of potatoes
4 garlic cloves in their skin
A pinch of salt
Black pepper, freshly ground
6 tbsps of extra virgin olive oil
2 sprigs of rosemary

DIRECTIONS
1. Peel the potatoes and cut them into small cubes.
2. Wash and drain the potatoes and pat dry with a clean teatowel or paper towel. Put the potatoes and the garlic cloves in a large oven dish. Season with salt, pepper and toss in the olive oil.
3. Add the rosemary twigs, tucking them under the potatoes so they don't burn. Bake in the oven at 220°C/425°F/Gas Mark 7 for about 25 minutes or until soft and golden.

INSALATA DI PATATE

These potatoes are served cold and are delicious with any of the meat courses.

Serves 4

INGREDIENTS
1kg of potatoes
30g fresh parsley
4 tbsps of vinegar
4 tbsps of extra virgin olive oil
A good pinch of salt to taste
Freshly ground black pepper

DIRECTIONS
1. Boil the potatoes in their skin until tender. They are ready when you can pierce them with a fork. Drain and cool. Peel them and cut into small cubes. Put in a bowl and add all the ingredients. Mix together gently and serve as a side order, cold like a salad.

BROCCOLI RIPASSATI

Now, we're moving to the south of Italy where broccoli is used in a lot of recipes. This is a very tasty, spicy recipe and is great for a side dish.

Serves 4

INGREDIENTS
Salt
600g of broccoli florets
2 garlic cloves, peeled
Dried red chilli, a pinch
Extra virgin olive oil

DIRECTIONS
1. Boil 2 litres of water with 25g of salt. Put the broccoli in the boiling water and, from when the water starts to boil again, leave the broccoli to cook for 4/5 minutes. Drain well.
2. Oil a pan, making sure that it is large enough to accommodate the broccoli. Add the garlic, chilli and cooked broccoli. Fry the broccoli, stirring constantly and being careful not to overcook it.
3. Serve the broccoli on its own or as a side dish to go with meat or fish.

FUNGHI TRIFOLATI

Serve this recipe as a side dish or as a very good topping to dress a *bruschetta*. The variety of mushrooms is up to you. You could use the classic button mushroom on its own (as we do in this dish) or add *porcini* or field mushrooms to elevate this dish to a new level.

Serves 4 as a side dish or for *bruschetta*

INGREDIENTS
500g button mushrooms
Extra virgin olive oil
2 garlic cloves, peeled, halved and stem removed
20g parsley, finely chopped
Salt and freshly ground black pepper
Nutmeg

DIRECTIONS
1. Let's start with the mushrooms. Wipe them clean with a damp cloth (please don't wash them as it ruins the texture). Cut them into thin slices.
2. Add the olive oil to the pan. Add the garlic and fry for a minute or two until golden. Remove the garlic and discard.
3. Add the mushrooms and cook them over a high heat, stirring them regularly. After a few minutes the mushrooms will start to release their water. Add half the parsley, a good sprinkling of salt, a grinding of pepper and just a hint of nutmeg. (If you don't like the idea of the nutmeg, you can leave it out. But I can guarantee that this will give a personal touch to this dish.)
4. Cook the mushrooms for less than 10 minutes, just enough time to allow the mushroom water to evaporate. Dress the mushrooms with olive oil and the remaining parsley.

TIRAMISÙ'

Tiramisù' is one of the most discussed Italian desserts. Everyone has their own recipe. There are people that use *marsala* or rum or *Vin Santo*. Only use the freshest free-range eggs for this recipe.

Serves 8-10

INGREDIENTS
7 medium eggs (60g each), separated
7 tbsps of sugar (120g)
700g of *mascarpone*
2 pinches of salt
400g *savoiardi* biscuits
300ml of tepid coffee
25g dark chocolate powder

DIRECTIONS
1. Whisk the yolks with half of the sugar until they are light and fluffy. In another bowl whisk the *mascarpone* to make sure that there are no lumps and add it to the fluffy yolk and sugar mixture.
2. In another bowl whisk the egg whites with a pinch of salt, adding the remaining sugar and whisking until stiff. With a wooden spoon fold in the egg white to the *mascarpone* using a figure eight movement. Now you have the cream for your *Tiramisù'*.
3. Get a large serving dish ready. Dip each *savoiardi* biscuit in the coffee. Make sure they are not too soaked because if they release liquid, your *tiramisù'* will be very soft. Make a layer of biscuits on the bottom of your dish. Cover the first layer with the cream and dust with the chocolate powder. Repeat, finishing with a later of cream and a dusting of chocolate powder.

PANNA COTTA

This is an easy recipe to get an exceptional result. People say our *panna cotta* is the best they have ever tasted, including other chefs!

INGREDIENTS
350g cream
35g sugar
1½ gelatine leaves
70ml *espresso* coffee, cold
Some coffee powder

DIRECTIONS
1. Bring the cream to the boil with the sugar (stir to dissolve the sugar).
2. Soak the gelatine in a bowl with cold water. When the gelatine is soft, remove and squeeze it and add it to the cream and sugar mixture.
3. Strain the cream and add the *espresso* coffee. Now divide your *panna cotta* mixture in cups or glasses and leave it in the fridge for at least 4 hours. Before you serve it, dust the top with a little coffee powder.

If you want to make another flavour of *panna cotta*, remove the coffee from the recipe above. Instead, add the seeds of half a vanilla pod to the hot cream and sugar mixture. The rest of the procedure is the same. You can garnish your *panna cotta* with some black forest fruits as we have in our photograph or with chocolate shavings.

TORTA NUTELLA E PERE

FOR THE DOUGH
125g butter at room temperature
125g sugar
A pinch of salt
1 tsp lemon zest
1 tsp orange zest
A tiny pinch of seeds from a vanilla pod (just a hint)
2 yolks from medium eggs
250g plain flour (00 flour works perfectly)

FOR THE FILLING
450g of Nutella
3 nearly ripe pears, cored but leave the skin and cut each pear into slices
Some icing sugar

1. Preheat the oven to 180ºC/350ºF/Gas Mark 4.
2. Mix the butter, sugar, salt, lemon and orange zest and vanilla at medium speed in a food-processor until well-combined. Add the eggs and increase the speed. Reduce the speed to medium and add the flour all together. Mix until the flour is combined (don't over mix or you will toughen the dough). Wrap the dough in cling-film and leave in the fridge for 1 hour. Dip the jar of Nutella in hot water to soften.
3. Grease a round baking tin with butter and dust with flour. Divide the dough into two. Roll out one portion to cover the base including the sides of the tin. Roll the second piece to fit the top. Lay the large piece of pastry in the tin and prick with a fork. Bake blind for 10 minutes. Remove from the oven, cover the base with pears and softened Nutella and cover with the pastry lid. Prick the pastry all over. Bake for another 10 minutes or until the pastry is cooked through.

TORTA RICOTTA E CIOCCOLATO

FOR THE DOUGH:
125g butter
125g sugar
Pinch of salt
1 tsp orange zest
A tiny pinch of seeds from a vanilla pod (just a hint)
2 yolks from medium eggs
250g plain flour (00 for pizza works perfectly)

FOR THE FILLING
250g fresh *ricotta* cheese
35g icing sugar and some for dusting
2 pinches of cinnamon
120g dark chocolate, cut into small pieces

DIRECTIONS
1. Preheat the oven to 180°C/350°F/Gas Mark 4.
2. Mix the butter, sugar, salt, orange zest and vanilla at medium speed
in a food-processor until well-combined. Add the eggs and increase the
speed. Reduce the speed to medium and add the flour all together.
Mix until the flour is combined. Wrap the dough in cling-film and chill.
3. Grease a round baking tin with butter and dust with flour. Divide the
dough into two. Roll out one portion to cover the base including the sides
of the tin. Roll the second piece to fit the top. Lay the large piece of
pastry in the tin and prick with a fork. Bake blind for 10 minutes.
4. Put the *ricotta* in a bowl and mix with sugar, cinnamon and chocolate.
Pour into the blind-baked pastry case. Cover with the pastry lid. Bake for
another 10 minutes or until the pastry is cooked through. Serve cold.

CHEESE PLATES

Serve a cheese plate after dinner (I prefer it instead of dessert) or eat one for lunch or a light dinner. Any of these cheese plates can be served on its own, or make up all the suggestions here for one cheese board.

MOZZARELLA AND BASIL

For a cheese plate, you can offer *mozzarella* and basil with some *mostarda*.

PARMIGIANO OR GRANA PADANO AND BALSAMIC

The *Parmigiano* or *Grana Padano* are usually grated in cooked dishes but here they can shine in their own right. The best way to cut *Parmigiano* is to run the knife halfway through, then bend the knife forwards and what you get is a nice shape of *Parmigiano* with crystals so when you eat it, you can feel the crunch. Buy a good *tradizionale* balsamic and match just a few drops with the cheese on each plate.

PECORINO AND PEAR

For me, *pecorino* and pear is the perfect match of sweet and salty. All types of *pecorino* are good, whether it is *Sardo*, *Romano* or *Toscano*. The pear must be ripe but not soft. Slice the pear just before serving.

GORGONZOLA AND CELERY

Serve the *Gorgonzola* with a celery stick which you use as a spoon to scoop up the soft cheese. You can also cut the celery into 2 inch pieces and fill them with room temperature *Gorgonzola* and top with walnuts.

HONEY

The best honey to serve with cheese is the chestnut honey because it is bitter but still sweet.

DIGESTIVI

In Italy, if it is a special occasion or if it is a Saturday or Sunday, we have a *digestif*. Most of the time in south Italy it is a *limoncello*. It's the most popular *digestif* abroad. We also drink *Amaro* which is made with bitter herbs to help digestion or *Grappa* which we use to 'correct' an *espresso* at the end of the meal. We pour a little of either into the *espresso* to make 'espresso corretto'. The best areas for *limoncello* are Sorrento (for the lemons which are world-famous) and Lake Garda.

VIN SANTO

Vin Santo means 'holy wine' and it was used during Mass in the past. We serve it at the end of the meal. It is made only in Tuscany and is an Italian dessert wine. The best way to drink it is to match it with the *cantucci* made with almonds. The *cantucci* are very hard to bite and when you dip them in the *Vin Santo*, it's much easier to enjoy them. It's made from the *Malvasia*

grape. Just a few producers make it and most of them do so using the original method. The *Vin Santo* is aged in a small barrel because they make a small quantity. It's important that it is also stored in a small bottle so you have to be careful when you find a large bottle of *Vin Santo* – it means that it is not of a good quality.

GLOSSARY

Soffritto is the equivalent of the french *mirepoix* of finely chopped vegetables which are cooked gently in olive oil to provide the bedrock of flavour to a dish. It is usually a mixture of onions, carrots and celery.

Mantecare is the important last step in the making of risotto. It is the loving gesture of adding butter and often, though not always, grated Parmesan, then stirring and leaving the risotto to rest for a short time to absorb it.

Contorno is the Italian equivalent for a 'side order'. In Italy it is served with a main course but it is never served with pasta and pasta is never served as an accompaniment to a dish.

Primo Piatto is the Italian for the pasta course which comes after the *antipasto* (or starter) and before the *secondo piatto* or main course of meat, fish or poultry.

Caffè e Ammazza caffè: This is a humorous way to order an *espresso* and a shot of liqueur at the end of the meal. The expression *Ammazzacaffè* means 'coffee killer' because the taste of the liqueur kills the flavour of the coffee.

Scarpetta means to clean the plate and if there is some sauce left to mop it up with the help of some bread. It's a way of showing you appreciate the food, something that is very important to Italians.

Aperitivo: In Italy the *aperitivo* consists of a glass of sparkling wine like *Prosecco, Franciacorta, Spumante* or a long drink made with vermouth like *Martini, Cinzano* or *Campari* or *Aperol*. It should be accompanied by finger food like olives, crisps, little sandwiches or perhaps nuts. An *aperitivo* should be taken before lunch or dinner.

ACKNOWLEDGEMENTS

OUR THANKS TO EVERYONE WHO HELPED TO MAKE THIS BOOK POSSIBLE

OUR SPONSORS:
Valter Citarella and famiglia Spadola from Caffè Moak {www.caffemoak.com}

Andrea Gradassi from Oleificio Gradassi {www.gradassi.com}

Michael Sullivan at Digiprint.ie {www.digiprint.ie}

TO EVERYONE WHO MADE OUR TRIP TO TUSCANY SPECIAL
– Silvia Formigli from Selezione Fattorie who arranged our visits to Godiolo,
Fattoria di Faltognano and Tringali {www.selezionefattorie.com}
– Franco Fiorini and everyone at Godiolo {www.godiolo.it}
– Count Roberto Comparini of Fattoria di Faltognano in Vinci {www.faltognano.it}
– Famiglia Tringali-Casanuova {www.tringalipro.it}
– Pieve de'Pitti {www.pievedepitti.it}

Thanks to Liezel Schultz who helped with the design of this book at all times of
the day and night and took every deadline to be absolute.

To Angela Tangianu, Director of the Italian Institute of Culture for her support.

Thank you to all the kind people in Italy who allowed us to take their photograph
and include it in our book.

To Laura who helped me many times, supported and put up with me always in the
background during this long viaggio. Marco
Diego, thanks for keeping me standing! Harry
To Colm for your blind faith. a.xx